# MARIA'S REAL MARGARITA BOOK

*by* **Al Lucero**

*Edited by* **John Harrisson**

**Ten Speed Press**

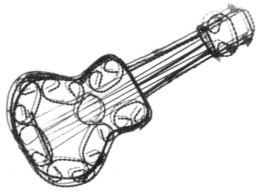

TEN SPEED PRESS
P.O. Box 7123
Berkeley, CA 94707

Cover and text design by Fifth Street Design, Berkeley, California
Photographs on page 4, 106, and first color insert by Michael Tincher
Photographs on page 9, 12, and 112 by Laurie Lucero
All other photography by Valerie Santagto

Library of Congress Cataloging-in-Publication Data

Lucero, Al.
    Maria's Real Margarita Book / Al Lucero
        p.   cm.
    Includes biographical references.
    ISBN 0-89815-640-8
    1. Cocktails. 2. Tequila. I. Title. II. Title: Real Margarita Book.
III. Title. Margarita book.
TX951.L793      1994
641.8'74—dc20                                          94-8404
                                                           CIP

Printed in the United States of America

First Printing 1994
1  2  3  4  5  —  98  97  96  95  94

# Contents

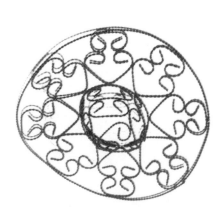

# Foreword

There was a time when a state of mind could be defined or cured by a good martini. It was a benchmark for a good time, a good lunch, a good date, a great place. The great American drink.

No more. Now, more often than not, in more places than most, that American measuring stick has given way to the new king: The Margarita. I don't know where or when or even how this started. I just know it's here. So now we hear about restaurants or bars defined by how great their Margaritas are.

What constitutes a truly great Margarita is not that easy to define. It is at once elusive and unforgiving. I once had a Margarita in Westport, Connecticut, and threw up an hour later. I've had watered down, oversweetened, too sour, and some a strange color. (Can there be a good strawberry Margarita?) One thing is certain. When you have a real Margarita, you know it.

When people have asked of a place to eat in Santa Fe, I find myself referring them to Maria's . Is it fancy? No. Is it chic? No. Is the food good? Yes. But the Margaritas – they are the best. When you read this book, you'll know why. Like anything of quality, it takes love and care, a degree of passion to execute it, love to start it, commitment to that love to sustain it. Maria's is a history and a definition. I am glad it's there. I'm glad I've tasted their Margaritas and I hope not too many people find out about it.

Robert Redford

# Maria's

I can remember first seeing the Maria's sign out front of the adobe-style building when I was about fourteen or fifteen years old, back in the early fifties. I was born and raised in Santa Fe, New Mexico and back then, a new restaurant was big news. The only others I can remember are the Pink Adobe, The Pantry, the El Gancho on the old Las Vegas Highway (now Old Pecos Trail), and a truck stop out on old Highway 85 (Cerrillos Road). Of course there was the La Fonda Hotel (a Santa Fe landmark) and I knew there was a "ritzy" restaurant inside, but it was only for adults and tourists with lots of money.

The state had just moved the old New Mexico state penitentiary south of town (having razed the old pen, which was located catty-corner to Maria's). Little did I imagine that the original owners of Maria's would be buying the used brick from the demolition of the pen to decorate the inside of a restaurant that I would, 30 years later, own.

Maria's is not only a historic Santa Fe landmark, it almost qualifies as a museum. The Cantina was built with used bricks from the old New Mexico State Penitentiary. The beer cooler is a converted icebox dating back to the 1880s which was shipped in from its perch in the old gold rush northern New Mexico town of Dawson. (My dad was a six-gun-toting Deputy U.S. Marshal in the area of Dawson at the turn of the century, so he could have easily had a couple of beers from that very ice box while it was still in its original spot.) The hand-carved and painted beams in the east room come from the old Public Service Company building in downtown Santa Fe. Much of the furniture throughout the restaurant is from the pre- World War II La Fonda Hotel. And on the art side, the famous Santa Fe artist, Alfred Morang, painted wall frescoes in the Cantina in exchange for food and drink. (We had these priceless paintings restored by local restoration experts who relished the thought of doing the job because of their admiration for Morang. Now dozens of other Santa Fe artists' work hangs on the walls of Maria's, as well.)

The Maria's tradition began in 1952 when Maria Lopez and her husband, Gilbert, started a take-out kitchen on the very same spot, in the very same building where Maria's exists today. As business boomed for the young Lopez couple, they slowly expanded, adding two booths and a patio.

Over the years, Maria's had its ups and downs. My wife Laurie and I are the fifth owners of Maria's. After moving back to Santa Fe in 1983 following a career as a

television executive (which took us all over the country), Laurie and I, like a lot of other couples, used to dine out a lot. We would critique each restaurant we visited and tell each other how we could have made it better. Relying on this great store of knowledge, we bought Maria's on December 1, 1985. We did however, have the benefit of history behind us: I am an umpteenth generation descendant of one of the old Spanish Conquistadors who captained an army which occupied Santa Fe in the 17th century — so my family has been cooking and eating New Mexican food for centuries.

Before we moved back to Santa Fe, we had really been looking forward to enjoying the wonderful New Mexican cooking at local restaurants. Unfortunately, once we got there we were quite disappointed. Some things had changed since I was a kid. Soupy beans and posole were being served on the plate with no broth. Tacos were being filled with roast beef and potatoes. Tortillas were all machine made. Margaritas were being poured out of slush-type machines, and so on. When we bought Maria's, we decided we were going to do things right. And we did. We served beans and posole in a bowl with broth, we made our tortillas by hand, and we introduced properly served fajitas to Santa Fe — which of course had to be accompanied by Margaritas!

Having researched other aspects of our restaurant to make sure that it was as authentic as possible, we were determined to make the best Margarita anywhere in the world! We studied up on tequila in Mexico and emphasized the quality and flavor of 100 percent agave tequila, mixing it with fresh, squeezed lemon juice and naturally-flavored triple sec, rather than manufactured sugar sweetened drink mixes. We found that it's amazing how fine a product can be made when you only use the best-quality ingredients available.

Our attention to detail and determination to make the best and purest Margarita possible have paid off. *The New York Times* called Maria's Margaritas the "best in town," *The Washington Post* said they are "world class," *Southwest Arts* described Maria's as "Margaritasville" and named our margaritas as one of the 101 reasons to visit Santa Fe. From *Better Homes and Gardens* to *Playboy Magazine,* newspapers and magazines nationwide, as well as almost every state and local publication, have given our Margaritas rave reviews.

Most Americans were raised drinking poor, or mediocre, tequila, whether straight or in a Margarita. The purpose of this book is to share the knowledge of how to recognize and appreciate a good tequila, and how to make the purest, most delightful cocktail on earth — the real Margarita!

¡Salud!

## Chapter 1

# Tequila

### *The Soul of a Real Margarita*

Y ou want a real margarita, right? Then it makes sense that you should use real ingredients to make it, especially real tequila. At Maria's in Santa Fe, we call our Margaritas "real Margaritas" because we use only real ingredients: real tequila, real triple-sec, and real lemon or lime juice. However, just because a bottle has the word *tequila* on its label does not automatically mean that it contains real tequila. So it's important that you learn the basic facts about tequila.

Tequila is an 80-proof liquor (40 percent alcohol by volume), that is made only in Mexico. It is double-distilled from the sugary juices extracted from the cooked *piña*, or heart, of the blue agave plant (*Tequilana weber*). And while there are 360 different varieties of agave, the blue agave is the only one from which tequila can be made. By the early 1990s, tequila had become the tenth best-selling spirit in the United States (vodka is the market leader). The United States not only imports more tequila than any other country in the world, it also consumes more tequila than Mexico. It is also the fastest-growing spirit in terms of sales, largely because of the ever-increasing popularity of Margaritas.

The Mexican government maintains strict control over the production of tequila and imposes exacting regulations on its distillers, the most important of which mandates that all tequila must be distilled twice, and must contain at least 51 percent blue agave sugar. Any product with less than 51 percent blue agave sugar cannot, by the Mexican government's standards, be considered tequila. So from now on we'll call tequila with 51 percent or more agave sugar "real" tequila and that with less than 51 percent agave sugar "unreal."

The use of the agave sugars in making tequila can best be described by comparing the manufacturing of tequila to the making of maple syrup. If one were to take the sap of a maple tree and add it to corn syrup it would not be pure maple syrup; it would be syrup with natural maple flavoring. Obviously, the higher percentage of the pure maple sap (sugar) used to make the syrup, the better maple flavor would result. The same chemistry applies to tequila. To be considered real tequila, no less than 51 percent pure agave sugar must be used with other neutral-flavored sugar (such as cane sugar) to ferment into the liquid that is then double-distilled to become the final 80-proof tequila. Obviously, the closer to 100 percent agave sugar used to make the tequila, the better the quality of the tequila.

Additional to the percentage of agave sugar, the Mexican government also requires that the agave plants used to make real tequila can only be grown in one of five Mexican states: Jalisco, Michoacan, Nayarit, Tamaulipas, or Guanajuato. Like fine Burgundy wines grown in different microclimates of adjacent valleys and mountainsides, there is a distinctive difference in flavor between tequilas (such as El Tesoro and Centinela) grown in the highlands of Jalisco around Arandas, and those (like José Cuervo) grown in the foothills near the village of Tequila, which is still the center of the tequila industry.

After the required 51 percent blue agave sugar, the remaining 49 percent (or less) liquid in tequila is generally cane sugar (usually Mexican-grown) and water, which is added to the blue agave sugar during fermentation. Some tequilas contain much more than the required 51 percent blue agave; however, only those tequilas that are 100 percent blue agave are required to list this percentage on the label. It is also required that each bottle of tequila (whether bottled in Mexico or elsewhere) carry the distiller's NOM (*Norma Oficial Mexicana*, or "official Mexican standard") number. This four-digit plus one-letter number is issued only to tequila distillers who can consistently pass government inspections and comply with the required regulations for the production of tequila. If a bottle of tequila does not have the distiller's NOM number on the label, it is not real tequila, even if the label says "Made in Mexico."

To appreciate premium tequila fully, it is important to understand that there are significant differences between premium tequila that merely complies with the Mexican government's minimum requirement of 51 percent blue agave and the best-quality super premium tequila distilled from 100 percent blue agave juice (known as *miel* in Mexico) with nothing else added.

All 100 percent blue agave tequilas must be bottled in Mexico and can only be exported in their original bottles. On the other hand, other tequilas can be and usually are exported in railroad tank cars or tanker trucks where it is then bottled at plants in various cities.

Both premium and super-premium tequilas come in several different grades. Here is where it gets interesting: different grades of tequila result in different kinds of Margaritas. The different types of tequila are categorized as *plata*, or *blanco* ("silver" or "white" tequila); gold; *reposado* ("rested," or aged for a brief time); *añejo* ("aged"); and *muy añejo* ("very aged").

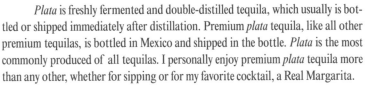

*Plata* is freshly fermented and double-distilled tequila, which usually is bottled or shipped immediately after distillation. Premium *plata* tequila, like all other premium tequilas, is bottled in Mexico and shipped in the bottle. *Plata* is the most commonly produced of all tequilas. I personally enjoy premium *plata* tequila more than any other, whether for sipping or for my favorite cocktail, a Real Margarita.

Gold tequila, also known as *joven abocado*, (translated as "young and smooth") is (are you ready to have your lifelong Jimmy Buffet image of tequila destroyed?) generally freshly distilled *plata* with caramel food coloring added to darken its appearance and give it an attractive golden hue. The Spanish word for gold, *oro*, is very seldom used in describing tequila; rather *añejo* or *muy añejo* is used. Aged tequilas may be gold in color also, but the color is the result of the aging process (the longer the aging the darker the color).

*Reposado* tequila is carefully aged in oak barrels for a minimum of two months and for no longer than one year. The color of the tequila will take on a little of the oaken tint from the wooden barrel, but sometimes the difference between *plata* tequila and *reposado* is almost indistinguishable. The "resting" processing enhances the flavor of *reposado* and may make the tequila a bit more mellow, but it

does not really affect the flavor of a Margarita. Most *reposado* tequilas are super-premium 100 percent agave tequilas.

*Añejo* tequila has been aged in oak barrels for a minimum of one year, a process that must be certified by the Mexican government. The color of *añejo* tequila varies, but most often it is a soft golden hue, not the deep gold of artificially colored "gold" tequilas. Almost all *añejo* and *muy añejo* tequilas are super premium tequilas.

*Muy añejo* tequila is aged in oak barrels for more than two years and, as with *añejo* tequila, the aging process must be certified by the Mexican government. Unlike whisky, tequila does not age well over long periods of time. As a matter of fact, tequila will reach its peak in oak in two to four years. If left on oak for five or six years, tequila is almost always "turned" (spoiled); much like bottled wine that has not been properly stored. However, once bottled, tequila will keep as well as most other distilled spirits and, like other spirits, finishes aging once removed from the oak barrels. The color of *muy añejo* tequila is naturally darker than the *añejo*, because it has been exposed to the oak wood longer; its coloring comes from the oak. *Muy añejo* is wonderful for sipping like a fine cognac, and it also creates a distinctive taste treat when used in a Margarita.

Two other Mexican liquors, mezcal and pulque, are sometimes confused with tequila. The one with the worm in the bottle is mezcal, which also is made from the blue agave plant, but is only distilled once. (The worm inside a mezcal bottle is actually the parasite which eats the roots of the agave plant.) Unlike tequila, mezcal is not inspected or regulated by the Mexican government. It is more like American moonshine — so be careful!

Pulque (pronounced pool-kae) could very easily be called the grandfather of tequila. It is the awful-tasting, undistilled fermented juice of the agave. Legend has it that centuries before the Spanish came to Mexico, lightning lit a wild agave plant on fire, cooking the *piña* and leaving its juices to ferment into a strong alcoholic liquid. The ancient Mexican Indians drank this liquid and as a result had great hallucinations which they reported to their priests. The priests then tried the *vino agave,* believed it allowed them to communicate with the gods, and proceeded to use the beverage for medicinal and religious purposes. Once the Spanish arrived and realized that the bitter juice was stronger than the wine they had brought with them, in an attempt to improve the flavor they distilled it — not once but twice. Hence tequila.

To this day, pulque is still sold and imbibed in Mexico, although it is likely that most of it is not actually made from the highly-coveted blue agave plant. There is no government control of pulque — so again, be careful!

As with fine wines, whiskies, or brandies (and a lot else besides), with tequila, you get what you pay for. You pay more for better quality. This means that 100 percent blue agave tequilas are more expensive. But, not to worry. You don't need super-premium tequila to make a real Margarita. After all, who can afford to have *Chateau Margaux* or *Opus One* with dinner every night? Don't count on using 100 percent agave tequila every time you have a margarita. Close to half of the Margaritas in this book, including Maria's Special, our house Margarita, use premium tequila. If you follow our recipes, you won't be disappointed.

# Chapter 2

# Other Essentials for a Real Margarita

*Liqueur, Citrus Juice, Salt, Ice, Equipment*

A real Margarita must contain three primary ingredients: real tequila, real triple-sec, real fresh-squeezed lime or lemon juice. It must also be correctly hand-shaken with ice, not put into a blender. Tequila drinks mixed in a blender, using extra sugar, concentrated lime juice or frozen lemonade, limeade, or a commercial Margarita mix, are not real Margaritas no matter how good the tequila is. Nothing bothers me more than to see a bar serving Margaritas out of a slush-type machine right into the glass (most likely made using a lot of ice, sugar, water, and cheap rotgut tequila). These are not real Margaritas!

T he variations among the Margaritas in this book are created by using different tequilas, different orange liqueurs, and different types of citrus juices to make a real Margarita.

## ★ The Liqueur ★

Margaritas are made using one of three different orange liqueurs: Triple-sec, Cointreau, or Grand Marnier. The combinations of different liqueur with the many different kinds of tequilas yield a wide variety of subtle variations on the basic Margarita.

Triple-sec is a clear liqueur made from the skins of Curaçao and other exotic oranges that have been fermented and then triple-distilled. Each of the distillations condenses the natural sugars and removes some of the bitterness of the orange peel. Most commercial triple-sec is artificially flavored; be sure to check the label to find one made with all-natural ingredients. Triple-secs are usually available in 60-proof or 42-proof. At Maria's we prefer the lower-alcohol content version with the delicate flavor of tequila. We use Bols brand 42-proof triple-sec for several of our Margaritas. Bols is a premium-quality triple-sec, as are Maria Brizard and DeKuyper.

Cointreau is a super-premium, 80-proof, orange liqueur imported from France. It was created in 1849 by Adolphe Cointreau and his brother Edouard who were candy makers experimenting with fruit and spirits. (It was probably the orange liqueur used to make the original Margarita.) Cointreau is a blend of bitter and sweet oranges, grown and selected for their quality in Haiti, Brazil, and Spain. The only part of the orange that is used is the peel which is laid out to dry in the sun for several days, and then sent back to the distillery in Angers, France. There the oil from the peels is blended with grain-neutral spirits and pure cane sugar and distilled three times. Cointreau's distinctive orange flavor is usually the best complement to premium or super-premium tequila. I wouldn't think of using anything other than Cointreau or Grand Marnier with super-premium tequila.

Grand Marnier, another French import, is made by blending super-premium orange liqueur with premium cognac that is then aged for a minimum of eighteen months. At Maria's, we use Grand Marnier to make our Grand Gold Margarita (see page 43), one of the most popular of all our Margaritas. Grand Marnier is 80-proof.

If you want a Margarita with a lot of character and a completely different "twist," make it with Grand Marnier. The subtle flavor of the oranges blends with the hint of the cognac and the flavor of the tequila to make quite a statement! However, because the flavor of the Grand Marnier can easily become the dominant flavor of the drink, Margaritas made with Cointreau are probably as authentic as you'll want to get. But you can decide what you like for yourself — there are an awful lot of folks that love Margaritas made with Grand Marnier.

## ★ The Citrus Juice ★

Based on research I have done on the origins of the Margarita (see Chapter 3), I am confident that the original Margarita was indeed made with freshly squeezed lime juice. Having said that, I must admit that we use freshly squeezed lemon juice at Maria's.

The reason we use lemon juice is that the quality of fresh limes is just too inconsistent. Depending on the season, we sometimes get limes from Mexico, at other times from California, Florida, or South America, and we are always at the mercy of our suppliers. Sometimes those limes can be so tart you can't stand them, while at other times they'll be as sweet as sugar. On the other hand, lemons are considerably more uniform in flavor, regardless of geographical origin or time of year. If you do find a sweet, juicy lime, we'll bet that you can tell little difference in flavor between a Margarita made with lemon juice and one made with lime juice. (We do not recommend frozen concentrated lime or lemon juice that has sugar added, but Minute Maid produces a pure, frozen unsweetened lemon juice that may be substituted for fresh.)

We never use commercial Margarita mix at Maria's and we strongly recommend that you avoid it too. We use a commercial sweet-and-sour mix in a Margarita only when a customer insists that his or her Margarita be frozen and mixed in the blender instead of shaken. The problem with using a blender to make Margaritas is that the ice turns to water and overdilutes the cocktail, making it almost flavorless. As convinced as we are at Maria's about what makes a real Margarita, we also believe that the customer is always right — even when he or she isn't.

## ★ The Salt ★

Salt is an important element of the Margarita. It is never put in the drink itself — it is only used on the rim of the Margarita glass. You simply pass a wedge of lemon or lime over the rim of an empty glass, then dip it in a saucer of salt.

We use kosher salt because it is additive-free and because the coarser texture has the best consistency. Simple table salt is acceptable, although you will need more of it and it will dissolve quickly. (If using table salt, use less lemon or lime juice on the rim of the glass so that less salt will stick to it.) Inexpensive boxes of kosher salt are available at most grocery stores and will last a very long time.

## ★ The Ice ★

One of the most important ingredients in a real Margarita is the ice. The shape and size of the ice cube is important, because as you shake the Margarita the corners of the ice cubes will break off and dilute the other ingredients to just the proper point. "Round ice cubes" are not only an oxymoron, they just don't work in a Margarita (they will work, however, if you crack each one). Be careful, as the more cracked and crushed your ice, the more diluted your Margarita.

You need to use small cubes, ideally about 1-inch square (a little smaller will do, but not too much larger than that). If you're using ice out of household refrigerator ice trays, crack it into pieces by tapping the cubes sharply with the back of a tablespoon while cradling them in the cupped palm of your hand. The ideal ice is the commercial type you buy in bags at most grocery, liquor, or convenience stores.

## ★ The Equipment ★

Real Margaritas are pretty low-tech and (you'll be glad to hear) require little capital investment. The first things you'll need are a stainless steel cocktail shaker top and a 16-ounce cocktail shaker.

Shaking the mixture of tequila, orange liqueur, lemon juice, and ice will break off just the right amount from the corners of the ice for proper dilution of the drink. For an "up" Margarita, strain the liquid only (without the ice) into a 9-ounce salt-rimmed saucer-bowl-type Margarita glass.

Please don't use a blender! All it does is purée everything into a watery slush, diluting the flavor of the tequila and the orange liqueur. The result is a pale version of a Margarita that bears little resemblance to the real thing and is a waste of good liquor. The one and only exception to this rule is when making fruit Margaritas. Although not true Margaritas, these are wonderful, refreshing summertime drinks, and sometimes you just can't beat the taste of fresh strawberries, peaches, or apricots. A blender or food processor is a must for making these; just follow the recipes we have provided.

We recommend that Margaritas be served "on the rocks," (over ice). We don't think you'll mind the little dilution that occurs during the time that it takes to consume your Margarita. The drink stays colder longer, and the water added from the melting ice will not affect the flavor of the Margarita.

If you prefer your Margaritas "up," or without ice, you'll need some sort of a drink strainer (you've probably seen one of those stainless steel things behind the bar that looks like a miniature Ping-Pong paddle with a spring around it). Some of the bartenders at Maria's prefer to strain Margaritas by inserting the bottom of the empty shaker top into the shaker glass with the cocktail mixture and pouring the liquid out into a glass. If you do this, you won't need a strainer (which makes it a cheap alternative).

We do not serve pitchers of Margaritas at Maria's for several reasons which involve the practical concerns of running a restaurant. For one thing, Margaritas are quite potent. Each one contains a double shot of 80-proof spirits in a drink so smooth and flavorful that when properly made it just goes down too easily. If we served entire pitchers of Margaritas, we would have a bunch of drunk customers and that is not our goal. Moreover, an entire pitcher of Margaritas sitting on a table would become so diluted from the melted ice that the intended flavor of the Margarita would be destroyed. With that in mind, the only feasible way to maintain the integrity of the Margarita's flavor in a pitcher would be to serve it with no ice in the pitcher. If you shook 8 Margaritas individually, and strained out the ice, a 64-ounce pitcher (most of our recipes yield about 8 ounces of liquid each) of one of our premium Margaritas would cost over $50.00 (there's not going to be a lot of takers).

We have had success serving numerous Margaritas at one time while maintaining the flavor by following a simple procedure using a large punch bowl. (We recently served our La Ultima Margarita to 1,000 people at the first annual Santa Fe Buckaroo Ball and received rave reviews!) To use a punch bowl, simply add a large chunk of ice (not cubes) after all of the ingredients are in the bowl and mixed well. Then stir to create a bit of melting. Using a ladle, pour the Margarita mixture into salt-rimmed glasses which have been filled at least three-quarters with ice cubes. The chunk of ice will add the proper amount of water to the concoction.

If you are entertaining at home and *do* choose to serve by the pitcher, you can hand shake individual Margaritas according to the recipe and strain off the liquid into a chilled pitcher until it's as full as you want it to be. Have an ice bucket handy, along with salted rim glasses. Add the ice to the presalted glasses and pour the Margarita from the pitcher.

We use two different types of glasses for our Margaritas. One is the hurricane style stemmed glass, which is curved like the glass chimney of hurricane lamps, and the other is the flat saucer-bowl-type stemmed glass often used for champagne. The hurricane glass is used for Margaritas on the rocks, and the saucer-bowl-type is used for "up" Margaritas.

Any variations of these glasses will do, and the Margarita Police will not hunt you down or press charges if you use a stemless glass. The main requirement is that your glasses be big enough to hold the Margaritas. As we like to put it: "It ain't what you drink from, it's what you're drinking" (or words to that effect).

The only other piece of equipment you will need is a jigger or other measuring device. All our recipes list the ingredients as ounces or fractions of an ounce (basic bar jiggers come in ¾-ounce, 1-ounce, 1½-ounce, and 2-ounce sizes). We recommend that you buy a combination stainless steel jigger with one side measuring ¾ ounce, the other

1¼ ounces (you can double the ¾ ounce side for 1½ ounces, etc.). These jiggers look like hour glasses and should be available at most gourmet cooking or bar supply outlets. If all else fails, just remember that ¾ ounce equals 1½ tablespoons and 1¼ ounce equals 2½ tablespoons.

# Chapter 3

# The Noble Origins of the Margarita

**W**ho invented the Margarita? One might just as easily ask, "Who discovered fire?" The point is, someone, sometime, took the plunge and made a Margarita. And, while not as old as fire, its flavor is unique unto itself.

There are several stories (or legends, if you will) as to the origin of the Margarita. In order to cover all the bases, we asked a number of food and beverage magazines to print a request for readers' versions of the Margarita story. We were surprised both by the number of responses, and by the variety of theories out there. Far be it from us to say which story is true; instead, we would like to pass along the most interesting stories so you can come to your own conclusion. The accounts are given in their original versions.

The most commonly related story of the Margarita's origin is this one:

> Shortly after World War II, corporate America (and Hollywood) discovered Palm Springs, California, as a pleasant and scenic retreat from the hustle and bustle of the big city: play some golf, talk some business, and enjoy some good liquor with the boys. Well, Palm Springs is only a few hours drive from Mexico and, with this close proximity, a magical "new" liquor, tequila, was discovered by affluent America.

> These corporate guys were introduced to tequila the old-fashioned way: a shot of tequila, a lick of salt, and a bite of lime — brings tears to your eyes, doesn't it? The same "good old boys" then started bringing their wives and girlfriends (and no doubt, in some cases both) to their little getaway out in the middle of the California desert and, like most men, they wanted to impress the womenfolk with their newly discovered tequila and their macho way of drinking it. Sorry, boys: the shot of tequila, lick of salt, and bite of lime wasn't the ladies' cup of tea.

> So along came Jones or Garcia (or whomever — history does not record the creative genius in this version) and concocted a drink that had all of the same elements of the shot of tequila — the liquor, the salt, and the lime — except that Cointreau was added to give the cocktail a little sweetness. This enterprising mixologist created the first Margarita by shaking the essential ingredients in a shaker glass over ice, then straining the cocktail into a salt-rimmed glass.

> Not only did the women love it, so did the guys. Although this legend does not name the bartender responsible, it does record that he named his creation after his girlfriend, Margarita. Or, who knows — perhaps the bartender was named Margarita!

Another theory submitted by an advertising agency (published in the Fall 1991 edition of the Taylor/Christian Advertising Agency magazine, *!deas*) identifies a specific woman named Margarita. You probably will not be too surprised to learn that Taylor/Christian Advertising was the agency of record for Cointreau when they published this story:

> According to legend, it was during a party at her [Margarita Sames] cliffside hacienda in Acapulco in 1948 when Margarita began experimenting with "the drink." Cointreau was the key ingredient, and today she scoffs at recipes that call for triple-sec. At the party was a group of her closest friends, among them Nicky Hilton of the Hilton Hotel legacy. . . . Margarita was looking for something to cut the dust of a hot December afternoon in Mexico when she stumbled upon "something that kept the party going for two weeks." Margarita's original recipe called for three parts of tequila to one part Cointreau and one part lime juice, but being cognizant of America's concern with alcohol, the agency asked her for permission to weaken the mixture. "Okay. As long as you

July 13, 1948

Dear Mr. Lacero,

Greetings from Acapulco! Sorry you can't be with us now to enjoy the sunny weather.

Here's a little memento to let you know I'm thinking of you and to tell you about this wonderful new concoction I created. I hope you'll try it yourself. It's delightful! When you taste it, I'll bet you'll feel like you're here.

Last Christmas, I wanted to give my guests something new and very special, so I mixed equal parts of Cointreau (my favorite liqueur), my best tequila and lime juice and served it in champagne glasses with just a dusting of salt on the rims. Everyone raved about "the drink," and how the smooth orange flavor of Cointreau blended with tequila and tart lime juice made a very refreshing cocktail. They all said they'd never tasted anything like it. It just made our holiday celebration!

The best part is that just last week, my husband Bill said we can't call it "the drink" forever, so he presented me with two lovely glasses etched with "Margarita." "Now 'the drink' has a name," he said. Wasn't that sweet?

Try my original, The Original Margarita made with Cointreau. I'm sure you'll find it as special as we all do.

Fondly,
Margarita

P.S. Keep the frame on your desk to remind you of the special times you'll always have with The Original Margarita.

*don't use triple-sec or blend it up like a Tastee Freeze," she replied tersely. To enjoy Margarita's original Margarita, blend one part tequila, one part fresh lime juice, and one part Cointreau in a shaker of ice. Shake vigorously and pour into a lightly salted glass. Anything else is not the Sames. And, according to Margarita, "not worth its salt!"*

We heard directly from the folks at Cointreau when they learned about our quest for the origin of the Margarita, and they sent us the preceeding letter. (Note the date of the letter — clever, huh? Especially since we sent out our call for Margarita legends in 1993! Whether the contents of the letter are true or not, you have to admire Cointreau's enterprising publicity department!)

An article from the July 1991 *Texas Monthly* (submitted by Patrick O'Rourke of Rémy Amerique in Sacramento, California — the U.S. distributor of Cointreau) discusses Mrs. Sames's claim. It also mentions that the owner of the Los Angeles restaurant and bar, the Tail o'the Cock, was a houseguest of Mrs. Sames, hence the theory that the Margarita originated there. (The Tail o'the Cock has also been mentioned in other Margarita-origin stories.)

This Associated Press obituary, submitted by Evelyn Greenwald of the Los Angeles Public Library's State of California Answering Network, appeared in newspapers all over the country in October 1992:

> Dateline: San Diego (AP) — *Carlos Herrera, known locally as the man who topped a tequila concoction with salt and called it a Margarita, has died. He was 90. Herrera died Monday at Grossmont Hospital. He had moved to San Diego from Tijuana, Mexico, five years ago. His daughter, Gloria Amezcua, said he died of natural causes. Herrera's relatives say he invented the drink at Rancho La Gloria, a restaurant he opened in 1935 at his home south of Tijuana. He told friends that it was sometime in 1938 or '39 that he decided to mix a jigger of white tequila with lemon juice, shaved ice, triple-sec and — the crowning touch — salt. Local legend has it that one of his customers was a showgirl and sometime actress who called herself Marjorie King. She was allergic to all hard liquor except tequila, and she didn't like to drink that straight. That reputedly set Herrera to experimenting, and he named the result "Margarita" after the actress, the legend goes.*

The above obituary was picked up and embellished by the Santa Rosa *Press Democrat*, which printed a feature story on the subject on May 14, 1992. The piece, submitted by Barbara Eck of Santa Rosa, California, reprinted AP's report of Herrera's death and his place in cocktail history as the inventor of the Margarita. It included this information:

Although Herrera was given local credit for the frosty drink, several others have claimed invention of the Margarita, according to *The Dictionary of American Food and Drink* by John F. Mariani, published in 1983.

The book doesn't name Herrera, but it says one story traces the birth of the Margarita to an unidentified creator near the Caliente Racetrack in the 1930s, the place and time Herrera claimed he first mixed a Margarita. (Hmmm. . . we wonder if Mr. Herrera ever worked at a bar at the Caliente Racetrack or in Palm Springs.)

We also thank Thomas Kandziora, the bar manager of the American Legion Post #288 in Cedarburg, Wisconsin, who sent us an abridged version of the article from the *Chicago Tribune,* and Mary Louise Rogers of San Diego who sent a similar article which ran in the *San Diego Tribune.* Mary Louise adds:

I believe this story must have some merit as I remember after arriving in San Diego late in 1958, friends and I made the trek to Rosarito Beach for lobster. There was a favorite bar we stopped at on the old road on our way down, and that was where I first drank a Margarita.

Food writer Colman Andrews sent us this contribution regarding the origin of the Margarita:

*I think I know what inspired it: the classic '30s cocktail called the Sidecar. The Sidecar was supposedly invented in 1931 at the legendary Harry's New York Bar on the Rue Daunou in Paris. The story is that it was created, and named, for a young American millionaire — there always seems to be a young American millionaire involved in tales of this sort — who liked to tour the drinking places of the French capital in the sidecar of a friend's motorcycle.*

*As you may well know, the Sidecar is classically made with two ounces of cognac, a half-ounce of fresh-squeezed lemon juice, and a quarter-ounce of Cointreau. These ingredients are shaken together with cracked ice and strained into a cocktail glass whose rim has been dipped in sugar. By simply replacing the cognac with tequila and the sugar with salt, you'd have a pretty reasonable Margarita — and I'd bet that some old-school bartender who knew the Sidecar, and who perhaps had traveled to Mexico where tequila might otherwise be consumed with salt and lime on the side, put various elements together and came up with this classic drink.*

*I have several cocktail manuals from the 1950s, incidentally, in which neither the Margarita nor tequila itself is mentioned, suggesting that, whenever it might have been invented, it certainly hadn't yet become a standard drink at that time in the United States. Though I'm sure it was around before this, the earliest reference I can find to it in my own library is from the Time-Life volume,* Wines and Spirits, *published in 1968. You might be amused to hear that, in the course of describing the drink, author Alec Waugh states, "Tequila is not a drink that is ever very likely to be popular*

*among Northerners, whose palates have not been hardened by the unrestrained use of chili. . . ."*

Nicholas Colletti of Pittsburgh, a keen collector of food facts, wrote to us with his theory about the origin of the Margarita:

*The Margarita was invented by Red Hinton, a bartender in an early Virginia City bar. He named the drink after Margarita Mendes, his Mexican girlfriend. One day, she hit a man over the head with a bottle of whiskey, and his friend, Robert Arthur, got excited and shot off his revolver to scare her away. He accidentally hit her in the top of the head and killed her. However, he was freed, as it was decided that if he had wanted to kill her, he would have aimed at the area that was easiest to hit — her widest area — which in her case happened to be her chest.*

*The recipe for the original Margarita was as follows: Wet the rim of a glass with the juice of a lemon. Place the rim in a bowl containing salt so the salt sticks to the rim. Put 1 ounce of tequila in a shaker or bowl. Add ½ ounce lemon juice and ½ ounce orange juice. Mix well and pour into the glass. There was no triple-sec or ice used to make this drink; there wasn't any in Virginia City when this drink was invented.*

Margee Drews from Corona Del Mar, California, wrote to tell us:

*I have heard many times that Larry J. Cano, former owner and President of El Torito restaurants, "invented" the blended Margarita as we know it. I've heard that he and a bartender, Barry, blended up a batch in a "slush" type machine. That was over thirty years ago in Los Angeles.*

[Sorry, Margee — that's not a real Margarita; it's a slushi!]

The following information, submitted by Raymond Ritter of Westlake, Ohio, is from *The Tequila Book* by Marion Gorman and Felipe P. de Alba (Contemporary Books, Inc., 1978). One of the theories given regarding the origin of the Margarita claims that Danny Negrete, the manager of the Crespo Hotel in Puebla, Mexico, created the drink in 1936 for his girlfriend, Margarita.

*She habitually took a dab of salt with whatever she had to drink. Danny decided that he would create a drink for her so she could enjoy it without having to reach into the common table salt-bowl; he would put the salt on the rim of her glass. He chose tequila — probably that was Margarita's favorite drink. Then he decided to add Cointreau and lemon [sic] juice and shake it up with ice.*

Another theory from the same source names Doña Bertha, the owner of a bar in Taxco, Mexico, as the creator of the Margarita.

Former Santa Fe restaurateur Walt McDowell wrote to us from Fort Myers, Florida, with a colorful and historical theory.

*The sixteenth century explorer, Ponce de Leon, traveled to the New World in search of the Fountain of Youth, said to be guarded by a race of ageless giants, the Calusa. While the Fountain of Youth was a myth, the Calusa were indeed a tribe that existed in Florida, and who were both tall (over six feet) and lived to an estimated eighty to ninety years of age. It is documented that the Calusa, who were trading partners with the Mayan civilization of Mexico, were versed in the cultivation of many tropical fruits, including sweet limes.*

*In 1513, Ponce de Leon made contact with the Calusa but later died in a war he fought against them. Two hundred years later, Ponce de Leon's direct descendant, Margerete, was the wife of a well-known pirate, Don José Gaspar, whose trading booty in the Gulf of Mexico included "cactus whisky," distilled from the agave plant and now known as tequila. Gaspar's favorite drink was sweet lime juice and "cactus whiskey," with a touch of sea salt left on the rim of the mug after it had been washed in sea water. This potion was named by his crew after his wife, Margerete.*

Elaine Corn, aptly-named food critic, writer, and author, wrote to let us know about Francisco "Pancho" Morales, a bartender from Juarez who claimed to have invented the Margarita in July 1942:

*He [Morales] plied his trade at Tommy's Place, a spot popular with Fort Bliss GIs. This is where the Margarita supposedly first was poured, despite claims to its origin as frequent as Elvis sightings.*

*The first thing to dispel is this: It wasn't named for a woman or child. A 1974 article in* Texas Monthly *magazine written by El Pasoan Brad Cooper ought to have been the last word on the subject, so thorough is the depiction. Pancho Morales is presented as the clear creator, with paper documentation, convenient timing, and oral testimony. Still, Cooper carefully constructs his article liberally using the term "supposedly" in almost every reference to anything having to do with the Margarita. . . .*

*"A lady came in and ordered a Magnolia," Morales told Cooper. The only thing Morales knew about a Magnolia — a true drink known in Juarez bars — was that it had Cointreau, a little lime and some kind of liquor. So, he did what any good bartender would do: He winged it.*

*The woman recognized the fake, but said it was good anyway, probably because Morales had loaded it up with enough tequila to make anyone smile. Morales's train of thought had gone to flowers, from magnolia to daisy, which translates in Spanish to Margarita.*

The following story was submitted by Ronnie Vaughan, a sales executive for the Albuquerque distributor of José Cuervo tequila. It's from the Cuervo "fact-book" provided to salespeople for the National Distributing Company:

> Margaritas originated "in heaven," say its most devoted admirers. Other versions of the story vary. One of the best claims has been staked by the Tail o' the Cock restaurant on La Cienega Boulevard in Los Angeles. The year: 1954. The culprit: the head bartender. The result: if this was indeed the first, a place in beverage history.

A similar story was provided by Lee Spencer:

> After the war, Young's Market Company owner Vernon Underwood owned a tequila brand called José Cuervo. They were and still are a major liquor distributor in Los Angeles. At that time, vodka was starting to move due to a popular drink made famous at the Cock and Bull restaurant on Sunset Boulevard, Los Angeles, called Moscow Mule. Underwood took his tequila to his friend McHenry, who owned the Tail o' the Cock restaurant. They gave it to his bartender, who put together a concoction using lime juice and Curaçao. The results were great, so now a name was needed. They asked the bartender, who said: "My wife's name is Margaret. Why not call it a Margarita, Spanish for Margaret?" The rest is history.

An article submitted by Dennis Hamann, printed in a beverage trade magazine in 1969, mentions the same Vernon Underwood, then-president of Young's Market Company. In this version, Underwood was curious to know why the Tail o'the Cock restaurant on La Cienega was suddenly ordering five cases of tequila at a time, during a period when tequila sales were relatively dormant. He found that the bartender had invented the Margarita, using Underwood's Cuervo tequila, and that this cocktail was rapidly winning acclaim by word of mouth. As a result, Underwood's company launched the first tequila advertising campaign with the theme, "Margarita is more than just a girl's name," with emphasis on the fact that the jet set had taken to drinking Margaritas in posh surroundings wearing white ties and tails.

Another article submitted by Glen "The Bartender" Stewart, from Las Vegas, Nevada repeats the claim that Carlos Herrera (see page 28) invented the Margarita, and named it after a showgirl, Marjorie King (although in this version, Herrera's first name is Danny). The article then quotes Herrera as saying, "The Mexican bartender at the Tail o'the Cock in Los Angeles was a friend, and I told him how to make it [the Margarita]. . . . One day I walked in there and he said, 'Danny, look around. Everybody's drinking Margaritas.'"

Could this be the missing link between these stories?

There are probably two or three dozen more stories about how the Margarita was invented. You might even know one of them. One problem in pinning down the origins of the Margarita is that, whatever you name the drink, tequila mixes so naturally and appealingly with citrus juices that it was bound to happen sooner or later, and perhaps sooner even than we think. The bottom line is, the Margarita *was* invented and, with some variations, it is the same (or we think it is the same) as it has been since the late 1930s (or late 40s, depending on who you believe). It is significant that the one common denominator in all the Margarita stories is the fact that no sugars are ever used, only unsweetened citrus juices. Regardless of what type of Margarita you're making, the sweetness should consist solely of the natural sweetness of the blue agave nectar that has been fermented and double-distilled into tequila and the orange liqueur that is mixed with it.

# Chapter 4

# Recipes for Real Margaritas

The Margarita recipes in this chapter are organized by tequila manufacturer and then by type. For example, we begin with Margaritas made with Cuervo tequila, from the mass-market Cuervo Silver up to the premium Cuervo Tradicional Reposado. Then we present Margaritas made with Sauza tequila, from Sauza Silver to Sauza Hornitos Reposado, and so on. The Margarita recipes at the beginning of this chapter use premium tequila, while those toward the end use super-premium tequilas.

T he recipes in this chapter feature virtually all of the real tequilas currently available on the American market. In some cases we use the same tequila for two Margarita recipes, altering the taste of the drink by changing the orange liqueur. You will note that some brands of tequilas are used in far more recipes than are others. This is due to the popularity of the tequila in the Margaritas at Maria's. While all of our Margaritas are real, not all are in an equal state of demand.

Each section begins with a brief discussion of the tequila manufacturer and the various tequilas under that name. Information on the specific tequila used in each Margarita appears in the headnote for each recipe. In addition, a glossary (at the back of the book) summarizes the pertinent facts and the resource list provides a source in case a certain tequila is unavailable in your local liquor store.

## ⋆ List of Real Margaritas ⋆

### ⋆ Cuervo
Maria's Special Margarita
The Cuervo Gold Margarita
The Rafael Margarita
The 1812 Overture Margarita
The Grand Gold Margarita
The Dos Reales de Plata Margarita
The Golden Coins Margarita
The José Cuervo Tradicional Margarita

### ⋆ Sauza
The Sauza Silver Margarita
The Sauza Gold Margarita
The Three G's Margarita
The Horny Toad Margarita
The Sauza Conmemorativo Margarita

## ★ La Viuda Romero/Real Hacienda
The Silver Widow Margarita
The Merry Widow Margarita
The Silver Lining Margarita
The Hacienda de Maria Margarita
El Gran Hacienda de Oro Margarita

## ★ Hussong's
Hussong's Special Margarita

## ★ Herradura
The Silver Herradura Margarita
The Santiago Margarita
The Herradura Gold Margarita
The Herradura Añejo Margarita

## ★ El Viejito
El Viejito Margarita

## ★ El Tesoro
The Elizabeth II Margarita
Maria's Famous La Ultima Margarita
The Grand Platinum Margarita
The Grand Treasure Margarita
La Margarita del Joven Estebán

## ★ Patrón
La Margarita de la Patróna
The Don Roberto Margarita

## ★ Centinela
The Centinela Reposado Margarita
The Silver Sentinel Margarita
The Blue Angel Margarita
The Hundred Grand Margarita
The Centinela Añejo Margarita
El Amor de Oro Margarita

# Cuervo

The name José Cuervo is virtually synonymous with tequila. Truly, Cuervo is the world's premier tequila distiller. They produce a wide array of premium and super-premium tequilas and export more than 1 million cases of tequila to the United States annually. Their Cuervo Silver is the number one best-selling tequila in the United States. (If your liquor or grocery store doesn't stock Cuervo, it's time to change stores!)

# Maria's Special Margarita

### Makes 1 Margarita

*Maria's Special Margarita is made with Cuervo Silver and is the number one best-selling hand-shaken Margarita in Santa Fe.*

✻

**1 lemon or lime wedge**
**Saucer of kosher salt (about ¼-inch deep)**
**1¼ ounces José Cuervo Silver tequila**
**¾ ounce Bols triple-sec**
**1½ ounces freshly squeezed lemon juice or lime juice**
**Ice**

✻

Run the lemon or lime wedge around the rim of a hurricane-style Margarita glass. Dip the rim of the glass into the saucer of salt, rotating the rim in the salt until the desired amount has collected on the glass.

Measure the tequila, triple-sec, and lemon or lime juice into a 16-ounce cocktail shaker glass full of ice. Place a stainless steel cocktail shaker over the glass, tapping the top to create a seal. Shake vigorously for about 5 seconds and pour into the salt-rimmed glass.

✻ *Margarita Tips Anytime you make a Margarita, consider the ice very carefully! Ice cubes should be no larger than 1 square inch (ideally 1 by 1½ inches thick) with corners. The corners will break off during the shaking and add the perfect amount of dilution for the drink. Round ice cubes are not the best. Most commercially sold ice cubes are your best bet when entertaining with Margaritas.*

✻ *Tequila Tidbit The United States is the biggest consumer of tequila, with imports more then double the consumption in Mexico itself.*

# The Cuervo Gold Margarita

Makes 1 Margarita

*José Cuervo Gold is perhaps the best known of all tequilas sold in the United States — it's the one that Jimmy Buffet refers to in his classic "Margaritaville" recording.*

✱

**1 lemon or lime wedge**
**Saucer of kosher salt (about ¼-inch deep)**
**1¼ ounces José Cuervo Tequila Especial (Premium Gold)**
**¾ ounce Bols triple-sec**
**1½ ounces freshly squeezed lemon juice or lime juice**
**Ice**

✱

Run the lemon or lime wedge around the rim of a hurricane-style Margarita glass. Dip the rim of the glass into the saucer of salt, rotating the rim in the salt until the desired amount has collected on the glass.

Measure the tequila, triple-sec, and lemon or lime juice into a 16-ounce cocktail shaker glass full of ice. Place a stainless steel cocktail shaker over the glass, tapping the top to create a seal. Shake vigorously for about 5 seconds and pour into the salt-rimmed glass.

✱ *Margarita Tips When you serve Margaritas using plastic glasses, use table salt instead of kosher salt as it sticks much better to the plastic. There's something about the coarser texture of kosher salt that just hates plastic!*

✱ *Tequila Tidbit A few tequila makers still grow, harvest, cook, and distill their own agave and wouldn't think of using any other agave. One such tequila is El Tesoro de Don Felipe (we refer to this brand as simply, "El Tesoro"), which is from the highlands of Jalisco in the Arandas area of Mexico. There, Don Felipe and his family select only the agave piñas which have reached proper maturity and harvest them for their estate grown, 100 percent agave tequila. The advantage: total quality control, from planting to cultivating to harvesting and eventual distilling and bottling (not unlike an estate-grown and -bottled Bordeaux by a French winemaker).*

# The Rafael Margarita

Makes 1 Margarita

*The Rafael, or "Ralph," is a long-time favorite of Maria's old-timers and was in fact named after a patron called Ralph who asked our bartender to make a Margarita according to this recipe. This Margarita differs from the earlier recipes by combining an inexpensive premium gold tequila (Cuervo Especial) with Cointreau, an expensive super-premium orange liqueur.*

✷

**1 lemon or lime wedge**
**Saucer of kosher salt (about ¼-inch deep)**
**1¼ ounces José Cuervo Especial Gold tequila**
**¾ ounce Cointreau**
**1½ ounces freshly squeezed lemon juice or lime juice**
**Ice**

✷

Run the lemon or lime wedge around the rim of a hurricane-style Margarita glass. Dip the rim of the glass into the saucer of salt, rotating the rim in the salt until the desired amount has collected on the glass.

Measure the tequila, Cointreau, and lemon or lime juice into a 16-ounce cocktail shaker glass full of ice. Place a stainless steel cocktail shaker over the glass, tapping the top to create a seal. Shake vigorously for about 5 seconds and pour into the salt-rimmed glass.

✷ *Margarita Tip As we progress with the Margarita recipes in this book, you will notice that while the ingredients remain proportionately consistent, the combinations of ingredients subtly change. For example, we not only use different tequilas, but different combinations of triple-sec, Cointreau, and Grand Marnier.*

✷ *Tequila Tidbit Tequila is located 40 miles northwest of Guadalajara and has a population of 25 thousand. The name means "lava hill" in the Nahuatl Indian (Aztec) language, but these native people had vanished by 1656, when a Spanish settlement was permanently established. "Lava hill" refers to the fact that the town sits on the lower slopes of an extinct volcano. The silicate-based volcanic soil is ideal for growing the blue agave plant.*

# The 1812 Overture Margarita

Makes 1 Margarita

*This Margarita derives its name from Cuervo's 1800 brand of tequila (what's twelve years between friends?) and the fact that this tequila, mixed with Cointreau, truly conjures up an overture of flavor. One of the most popular premium tequilas made by Cuervo, José Cuervo 1800 comes in a decanter-type bottle.*

✶

**1 lemon or lime wedge**
**Saucer of kosher salt (about ¼-inch deep)**
**1¼ ounces José Cuervo 1800 tequila**
**¾ ounce Bols triple-sec**
**1½ ounces freshly squeezed lemon juice or lime juice**
**Ice**

✶

Run the lemon or lime wedge around the rim of a hurricane-style Margarita glass. Dip the rim of the glass into the saucer of salt, rotating the rim in the salt until the desired amount has collected on the glass.

Measure the tequila, triple-sec, and lemon or lime juice into a 16-ounce cocktail shaker glass full of ice. Place a stainless steel cocktail shaker over the glass, tapping the top to create a seal. Shake vigorously for about 5 seconds and pour into the salt-rimmed glass.

✶ *Margarita Tip Because you are going to be the Margarita Maven in your circle of friends, invest in a small, 3-pound box of kosher salt; this will last a while and is sure to really impress your pals.*

✶ *Tequila Tidbit There are many popular songs that extol the virtues of tequila. In the 1950s, the Champs recorded "Tequila"; the Eagles are famous for their "Tequila Sunrise," and we've already mentioned Jimmy Buffet's "Margaritaville." There's also Bobby Bare's "Pour Me Another Tequila, Sheila," but perhaps while you sip this particular cocktail, you'd like to hum along with Shelley West's classic, "José Cuervo, You Are a Friend of Mine."*

# The Grand Gold Margarita

### Makes 1 Margarita

*We use the same Cuervo premium gold tequila for this recipe as for the previous Cuervo Gold Margarita, but Grand Marnier rather than triple-sec. This gives the cocktail a more intense, sweeter flavor.*

★

**1 lemon or lime wedge**
**Saucer of kosher salt (about ¼-inch deep)**
**1¼ ounces José Cuervo Especial (premium gold) tequila**
**¾ ounce Grand Marnier**
**1½ ounces freshly squeezed lemon juice or lime juice**
**Ice**

★

Run the lemon or lime wedge around the rim of a hurricane-style Margarita glass. Dip the rim of the glass into the saucer of salt, rotating the rim in the salt until the desired amount has collected on the glass.

   Measure the tequila, Grand Marnier, and lemon or lime juice into a 16-ounce cocktail shaker glass full of ice. Place a stainless steel cocktail shaker over the glass, tapping the top to create a seal. Shake vigorously for about 5 seconds and pour into the salt-rimmed glass.

★ *Margarita Tip* *To make an "up" Margarita, here's how the bartenders at Maria's do it: After shaking the cocktail, remove the steel shaker top from the glass shaker, tapping the shaker top gently with the palm of your hand if necessary to break the seal. Leave the mixture in the glass shaker and place the steel shaker top bottom-first into the glass, leaving just enough room around the edge of the steel shaker top for the liquid to escape and the ice to remain in the container. Always discard the used ice when making "up" Margaritas and use fresh ice for the next drink.*

★ *Tequila Tidbit* *Blue agave plants have very shallow roots; no more than 1 foot underground. The harvested plants average 40 to 80 pounds each.*

# The Dos Reales de Plata Margarita

Makes 1 Margarita

*Cuervo's excellent Dos Reales tequila, together with their Tradicional 100 percent blue agave tequila have made this producer an important player in the premium and highly coveted super-premium tequila market.*

✯

**1 lemon or lime wedge**
**Saucer of kosher salt (about ¼-inch deep)**
**1¼ ounces José Cuervo Dos Reales de Plata tequila**
**¾ ounce Cointreau**
**1½ ounces freshly squeezed lemon juice or lime juice**
**Ice**

✯

Run the lemon or lime wedge around the rim of a hurricane-style Margarita glass. Dip the rim of the glass into the saucer of salt, rotating the rim in the salt until the desired amount has collected on the glass.

Measure the tequila, Cointreau, and lemon or lime juice into a 16-ounce cocktail shaker glass full of ice. Place a stainless steel cocktail shaker over the glass, tapping the top to create a seal. Shake vigorously for about 5 seconds and pour into the salt-rimmed glass.

✯ *Margarita Tip Invite some friends over and compare the different flavors you are able to create by using Dos Reales de Plata tequila and interchanging the Cointreau with Grand Marnier or triple-sec. You can also experiment with substituting fresh lime juice for the lemon juice. Code the glasses for a blind tasting and keep score — it's always a good idea to keep the notes for future reference. Most important, appoint designated drivers in advance, if necessary.*

✯ *Tequila Tidbit All tequilas are double distilled. In the case of the 100 percent agave tequila, that means simply that the fermented agave juices (miel) are distilled once, then distilled a second time into a ready-to-drink, clear, fresh product which can be bottled as a white, or silver tequila immediately, or held in stainless steel tanks until the distiller is ready to bottle.*

# The Golden Coins Margarita

Makes 1 Margarita

*Cuervo introduced their Dos Reales Añejo tequila relatively recently. The label describes Dos Reales as "a tequila of unparalleled smoothness and quality. It is distilled from carefully selected agave plants and aged in oak barrels to achieve the perfect balance of taste and smoothness." The name Dos Reales, loosely translated, means "two bits," but, more figuratively, "two coins." This, along with the golden color of the añejo tequila, inspired us to christen this drink "the golden coins."*

**1 lemon or lime wedge**
**Saucer of kosher salt (about ¼-inch deep)**
**1¼ ounces José Cuervo Dos Reales Añejo tequila**
**¾ ounce Cointreau**
**1½ ounces freshly squeezed lemon juice or lime juice**
**Ice**

✶

Run the lemon or lime wedge around the rim of a hurricane-style Margarita glass. Dip the rim of the glass into the saucer of salt, rotating the rim in the salt until the desired amount has collected on the glass. (If using table salt, just moisten the rim lightly.)

Measure the tequila, Cointreau, and lemon or lime juice into a 16-ounce cocktail shaker glass full of ice. Place a stainless steel cocktail shaker over the glass, tapping the top to create a seal. Shake vigorously for about 5 seconds and pour into the salt-rimmed glass.

✶ *Margarita Tip You can, if you want, garnish your Margarita with a lemon or lime slice, but you really don't need to. In any case, don't use any other garnish as it will impart its taste to the masterpiece you've just created.*

✶ *Tequila Tidbit Some of the tequilas we find on the liquor store shelves in the United States are not available in Mexico — at least not under the name we know them by here. For instance, El Tesoro is bottled as Tequila Tapatio in Mexico.*

# The José Cuervo Tradicional Margarita

Makes 1 Margarita

*Cuervo, the leading tequila producer in the world, has now brought out a limited production of Tequila Cuervo Tradicional, a super-premium tequila reposado (aged in oak barrels for at least sixty days). It is wonderfully smooth, with a delightful nose and flavor.*

★

**1 lemon or lime wedge
Saucer of kosher salt (about ¼-inch deep)
1¼ ounces José Cuervo Tradicional Reposado tequila
¾ ounce Cointreau
1½ ounces freshly squeezed lemon juice or lime juice
Ice**

★

Run the lemon or lime wedge around the rim of a hurricane-style Margarita glass. Dip the rim of the glass into the saucer of salt, rotating the rim in the salt until the desired amount has collected on the glass.

Measure the tequila, Cointreau, and lemon or lime juice into a 16-ounce cocktail shaker glass full of ice. Place a stainless steel cocktail shaker over the glass, tapping the top to create a seal. Shake vigorously for about 5 seconds and pour into the salt-rimmed glass.

★*Margarita Tip* At Maria's, we have strong feelings about commercial Margarita mixes. Don't waste good money on them when the best you can use – fresh lemons or limes – costs only pennies per drink.

★*Tequila Tidbit* Each bottle of Cuervo Tradicional is individually numbered. Cuervo has bottled this fine tequila in 375 ml bottles. However, they are expected to begin bottling in the industry norm, 750 ml bottles, in the near future.

# Sauza

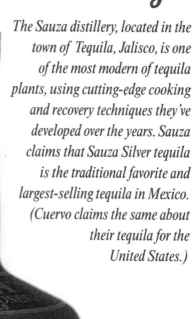

The Sauza distillery, located in the town of Tequila, Jalisco, is one of the most modern of tequila plants, using cutting-edge cooking and recovery techniques they've developed over the years. Sauza claims that Sauza Silver tequila is the traditional favorite and largest-selling tequila in Mexico. (Cuervo claims the same about their tequila for the United States.)

# The Sauza Silver Margarita

Makes 1 Margarita

*Tequila aficionados will debate whether Sauza Silver or Cuervo Silver is the best popular-priced tequila sold in the United States. Both are excellent products — I suggest you try both and decide for yourself (as if you need an excuse to taste-test!).*

**1 lemon or lime wedge**
**Saucer of kosher salt (about ¼-inch deep)**
**1¼ ounces Sauza Silver tequila**
**¾ ounce Bols triple-sec**
**1½ ounces freshly squeezed lemon juice or lime juice**
**Ice**

Run the lemon or lime wedge around the rim of a hurricane-style Margarita glass. Dip the rim of the glass into the saucer of salt, rotating the rim in the salt until the desired amount has collected on the glass.

Measure the tequila, triple-sec, and lemon or lime juice into a 16-ounce cocktail shaker glass full of ice. Place a stainless steel cocktail shaker over the glass, tapping the top to create a seal. Shake vigorously for about 5 seconds and pour into the salt-rimmed glass.

★ *Margarita Tip* *Attention all readers with a sweet tooth! The natural sugars in the ingredients listed in these recipes should be more than enough to satisfy even the sweetest of the sweet-toothed (sweet-teethed?). If you're used to drinking extremely sweet Margaritas, however, ours may seem a bit dry to you. But hey, these are Real Margaritas, so we urge you to try a few of our recipes. We are sure that you'll never stray back to icky-sweet fake Margaritas again!*

★ *Tequila Tidbit* *American vendors tend to rank liquor quality in terms of premium and super-premium. Tequilas which comply with the Mexican government's strict regulations, such as José Cuervo or Sauza tequila are considered premium, because they contain at least 51 percent agave sugars. The tequilas made from 100 percent agave sugar such as Herradura, El Tesoro and Centinela are considered super-premium.*

# The Sauza Gold Margarita

Makes 1 Margarita

*This Margarita is made with one of the most popular tequilas used in Mexico: Sauza Tequila Especial, Tipo de Oro ("gold type"). You'll notice that the most reputable distillers, like Sauza, will not try to mislead the public by calling a fresh tequila with caramel coloring añejo, which derives its golden color from aging on oak.*

**1 lemon or lime wedge
Saucer of kosher salt (about ¼-inch deep)
1¼ ounces Sauza Gold Tequila
¾ ounce Bols triple-sec
1½ ounces freshly squeezed lemon juice or lime juice
Ice**

★

Run the lemon or lime wedge around the rim of a hurricane-style Margarita glass. Dip the rim of the glass into the saucer of salt, rotating the rim in the salt until the desired amount has collected on the glass.

Measure the tequila, triple-sec, and lemon or lime juice into a 16-ounce cocktail shaker glass full of ice. Place a stainless steel cocktail shaker over the glass tapping the top to create a seal. Shake vigorously for about 5 seconds and pour into the salt-rimmed glass.

★ *Margarita Tip Using commercial ice cubes in your Margaritas will give you two advantages: they are crystal clear and they are usually made from filtered water.*

★ *Tequila Tidbit The very first tequila imported into the United States came to New Mexico in August, 1873. The shipment of 3 barrels and 6 bottles originated with Don Cenobio Sauza, whose company was to become the market leader, along with José Cuervo.*

# The Three G's Margarita

Makes 1 Margarita

*The "Three G's" in the title refers to Sauza's Tres Generaciones (Three Generations) Tequila Añejo, an aged tequila produced to honor the successive tequila makers of the Sauza family since 1873: Don Cenobio, Don Eladio, and Don Javier Sauza. This tequila, like all añejos, must be aged in inspector-sealed oak barrels for more than one year. Because of this, the tequila is a pale golden color that is acquired naturally from the barrels during the aging process.*

✶

**1 lemon or lime wedge**
**Saucer of kosher salt (about ¼-inch deep)**
**1¼ ounces Sauza Tres Generaciones Tequila Añejo**
**¾ ounce Cointreau**
**1½ ounces freshly squeezed lemon juice or lime juice**
**Ice**

✶

Run the lemon or lime wedge around the rim of a hurricane-style Margarita glass. Dip the rim of the glass into the saucer of salt, rotating the rim in the salt until the desired amount has collected on the glass.

Measure the tequila, Cointreau, and lemon or lime juice into a 16-ounce cocktail shaker glass full of ice. Place a stainless steel cocktail shaker over the glass, tapping the top to create a seal. Shake vigorously for about 5 seconds and pour into the salt-rimmed glass.

✶ *Margarita Tip Some bars serve Margaritas with a straw. Heck, we do at Maria's! The straw should be used to stir rather than for sipping the cocktail. Margaritas should be sipped from the rim of the glass, through the salt.*

✶ *Tequila Tidbit Most aged tequilas are placed in oak barrels (most often old, used Kentucky whiskey barrels) for the aging process. Mexican government inspectors seal these barrels when the tequila is put down and must be present when the seal is broken by the producer to bottle the product.*

# The Horny Toad Margarita

Makes 1 Margarita

*Horny toad is slang for "horned toad," a creature found in abundance in the high-desert terrain around Santa Fe. Maria's sells a lot of these Margaritas just because of the name (usually, the wife or girlfriend orders it while smiling at the husband or boyfriend and saying something like "BOY, was this one named after you!"). It also happens to be one of the best Margaritas at Maria's. "Hornitos" in Spanish means "little ovens" and refers to the ovens in which the agave piñas are cooked.*

★

**1 lemon or lime wedge**
**Saucer of kosher salt (about ¼-inch deep)**
**1¼ ounces Sauza Hornitos Reposado tequila**
**¾ ounce Cointreau**
**1½ ounces freshly squeezed lemon juice or lime juice**
**Ice**

★

Run the lemon or lime wedge around the rim of a hurricane-style Margarita glass. Dip the rim of the glass into the saucer of salt, rotating the rim in the salt until the desired amount has collected on the glass.

Measure the tequila, Cointreau, and lemon or lime juice into a 16-ounce cocktail shaker glass full of ice. Place a stainless steel cocktail shaker over the glass, tapping the top to create a seal. Shake vigorously for about 5 seconds and pour into the salt-rimmed glass.

★ *Margarita Tip Because of the alcohol content of Margaritas (see tip on page 52), we recommend eating something hearty to minimize the absorption into the bloodstream. If you drink more than a couple over a short period of time, please don't drive.*

★ *Tequila Tidbit Hornitos is one of Sauza's oldest and most venerable tequilas. It is a 100 percent blue agave tequila resposado (aged no less than 3 months and up to 1 year in oak barrels). Because of the slight aging, Hornitos reposado is slightly darker in color than the silver tequila, and as with most 100 percent agave tequila that has been aged, no artificial coloring has been added.*

# The Sauza Conmemorativo Margarita

Makes 1 Margarita

*Sauza tequila is the major rival to Cuervo, in terms of volume and market share, and the Conmemorativo brand was introduced in an attempt to compete with the premium tequilas that Cuervo has been placing in the American market. It is a delightfully smooth añejo tequila, and even though it is bulk-shipped to Greenwich, Connecticut, for bottling, it is difficult to tell that this tequila is not 100 percent blue agave.*

✴

**1 lemon or lime wedge**
**Saucer of kosher salt (about ¼-inch deep)**
**1¼ ounces Sauza Conmemorativo Añejo tequila**
**¾ ounce Cointreau**
**1½ ounces freshly squeezed lemon juice or lime juice**
**Ice**

✴

Run the lemon or lime wedge around the rim of a hurricane-style Margarita glass. Dip the rim of the glass into the saucer of salt, rotating the rim in the salt until the desired amount has collected on the glass.

Measure the tequila, Cointreau, and lemon or lime juice into a 16-ounce cocktail shaker glass full of ice. Place a stainless steel cocktail shaker over the glass, tapping the top to create a seal. Shake vigorously for about 5 seconds and pour into the salt-rimmed glass.

✴*Margarita Tip* *Tequila is 80-proof (the "proof" is double the percentage of the alcohol in liquor, so 80-proof means that 40 percent of the volume is alcohol). Triple-sec is usually 60-proof, but it can be 40-proof. Cointreau and Grand Marnier are both 80-proof. All this means that when you combine tequila with one of these liqueurs, you are actually serving a double — the same thing as serving a double-shot of 80-proof whiskey, for example. So consume Margaritas (like all other alcohol) responsibly and in moderation!*

✴ *Tequila Tidbit* *Only 100 percent agave tequila is required to carry that statement on the label. Any other tequila that is at least 51 percent agave does not have to state its agave percentage on the label. Some tequilas are obviously more than 51 percent agave, but you'll never know by just reading the label.*

# La Viuda de Romero/ Real Hacienda

Like many fine makers of tequila, La Viuda de Romero (Romero's Widow) distillery is located in the village of Tequila, Jalisco. It has been there since 1852. The super-premium brands of tequila from this distillery are imported under the name Real Hacienda — the entire line of which are 100 percent blue agave.

TEQUILA
100% DE AGAVE TEQUILERO

Real Hacienda

REPOSADO
6 MONTHS OLD
100% BLUE AGAVE TEQUILANA WEBER
Distilled & Bottled in the historic Village of
Tequila, Jalisco, México.
BY TEQUILA VIUDA DE ROMERO, S.A.
750 ml* 40% ALC./VOL. (80 PROOF)

# The Silver Widow Margarita

Makes 1 Margarita

*La Viuda de Romero is not a 100 percent blue agave tequila,*
*but it is produced and bottled in Tequila, Mexico. It's moderately priced*
*and makes a great Margarita!*

✷

**1 lemon or lime wedge**
**Saucer of kosher salt (about ¼-inch deep)**
**1¼ ounces La Viuda de Romero Plata tequila**
**¾ ounce Bols triple-sec**
**1½ ounces freshly squeezed lemon juice or lime juice**
**Ice**

✷

Run the lemon or lime wedge around the rim of a hurricane-style Margarita glass. Dip the rim of the glass into the saucer of salt, rotating the rim in the salt until the desired amount has collected on the glass.

Measure the tequila, triple-sec, and lemon or lime juice into a 16-ounce cocktail shaker glass full of ice. Place a stainless steel cocktail shaker over the glass, tapping the top to create a seal. Shake vigorously for about 5 seconds and pour into the salt-rimmed glass.

✶ *Margarita Tip Most Americans expect froth on a Margarita. If it's an authentic Margarita, using only the ingredients listed in these recipes, however, there will be little or no froth (although there may be a few bubbles on top of the liquid when it's poured into a glass). The froth on most cocktails is usually deliberately engineered by bartenders who use (surprise!) a frothing ingredient such as a powder made from egg whites or a mix that already includes ingredients specifically for this purpose. So remember, if you are drinking a frothy Margarita, it's not a real Margarita — and you are consuming additives that you don't need in your drink.*

✶ *Tequila Tidbit The maximum period for aging tequila in wooden barrels is 3 to 4 years. It is one spirit that does not improve with age. After 6 or 7 years in the barrel, tequila becomes unpalatable.*

# The Merry Widow Margarita

Makes 1 Margarita

*While the word "widow" may conjure up visions of somberly-dressed old ladies, the elegant woman who graces the label of Viuda de Romero doesn't fit this image at all — hence the name of the Margarita. Although there is a distinct agave flavor to this aged tequila, there is no 100 percent blue agave designation on the label.*

**1 lemon or lime wedge**
**Saucer of kosher salt (about ¼-inch deep)**
**1¼ ounces La Viuda de Romero Añejo two-year-old tequila**
**¾ ounce Bols triple-sec**
**1½ ounces freshly squeezed lemon juice or lime juice**
**Ice**

★

Run the lemon or lime wedge around the rim of a hurricane-style Margarita glass. Dip the rim of the glass into the saucer of salt, rotating the rim in the salt until the desired amount has collected on the glass.

Measure the tequila, triple-sec, and lemon or lime juice into a 16-ounce cocktail shaker glass full of ice. Place a stainless steel cocktail shaker over the glass, tapping the top to create a seal. Shake vigorously for about 5 seconds and pour into the salt-rimmed glass.

★*Margarita Tip* People have a tendency to serve Margaritas only with Mexican food. Next time you invest in a super-premium bottle of tequila, don't let it sit on a shelf waiting for your next fiesta. Try serving about 1½ ounces of 100 percent blue agave tequila in brandy snifters after dinner instead of cognac. Your guests will marvel at your good taste and sophistication.

★*Tequila Tidbit* Essential Spanish for the self-respecting tequilista:
Jimador or Mescalero — the agave field workers;
Piña — the heart of the agave plant used to make tequila;
Coa — the tool used to harvest the piñas.

# The Silver Lining Margarita

## Makes 1 Margarita

*The Real Hacienda line of super-premium tequilas consists of a 100 percent blue agave silver, reposado, and an añejo tequila.*

**1 lemon or lime wedge**
**Saucer of kosher salt (about ¼-inch deep)**
**1¼ ounces Real Hacienda 100 Percent Blue Agave Silver tequila**
**¾ ounce Cointreau**
**1½ ounces freshly squeezed lemon juice or lime juice**
**Ice**

✶

Run the lemon or lime wedge around the rim of a hurricane-style Margarita glass. Dip the rim of the glass into the saucer of salt, rotating the rim in the salt until the desired amount has collected on the glass.

Measure the tequila, Cointreau, and lemon or lime juice into a 16-ounce cocktail shaker glass full of ice. Place a stainless steel cocktail shaker over the glass, tapping the top to create a seal. Shake vigorously for about 5 seconds and pour into the salt-rimmed glass.

✶*Margarita Tip If you are having a party, or plan on serving Margaritas to a large group of people, you may want to pre-salt a number of glasses. The way we do it at Maria's (where we serve as many as 3 thousand margaritas in a week) is to place a clean, thin sponge on a saucer, and moisten it with fresh lemon or lime juice. Turn a glass upside down and press the rim down on the sponge to moisten it. Then dip the rim into a saucer of kosher salt and rotate the rim until the desired amount of salt has collected on the glass. Set the Margarita glasses upright next to the serving area.*

✶*Tequila Tidbit Some distillers will manufacture tequila for more than one importer. The one producer can sell his tequila to as many "brands" as he likes or as much as the traffic will bear. However, the producers' NOM number will remain the same on all the brands he produces.*

# The Hacienda de Maria Margarita

Makes 1 Margarita

*This Margarita uses the super-premium Real Hacienda 100 percent blue agave reposado tequila from Casa Viuda. The fact that we named this Margarita after our restaurant shows you that we think a lot of this tequila.*

**1 lemon or lime wedge**
**Saucer of kosher salt (about ¼-inch deep)**
**1¼ ounces Real Hacienda 100 Percent Blue Agave Reposado tequila**
**¾ ounce Cointreau**
**1½ ounces freshly squeezed lemon juice or lime juice**
**Ice**

Run the lemon or lime wedge around the rim of a hurricane-style Margarita glass. Dip the rim of the glass into the saucer of salt, rotating the rim in the salt until the desired amount has collected on the glass.

Measure the tequila, Cointreau, and lemon or lime juice into a 16-ounce cocktail shaker glass full of ice. Place a stainless steel cocktail shaker over the glass, tapping the top to create a seal. Shake vigorously for about 5 seconds and pour into the salt-rimmed glass.

★ *Margarita Tip If serving Margaritas at a party, always make unsalted glasses available for those who insist that salt is not good for them, as well as for guests who just prefer an unsalted rim.*

★ *Tequila Tidbit Mature agave piñas are harvested after 8 to 12 years. They range from 40 to 60 pounds each and are generally chopped into chunks by hand before they are placed into hornos (ovens), where they are steam-cooked for 24 to 36 hours. The cooked agave is similar to a cooked sweet potato in appearance, but is as sweet as sugar. The cooked agave is then crushed to remove the juice that will soon become tequila.*

# El Gran Hacienda de Oro Margarita

Makes 1 Margarita

*This Margarita uses an añejo tequila that definitely succeeds in balancing the flavorful Grand Marnier.*

✶

**1 lemon or lime wedge
Saucer of kosher salt (about ¼-inch deep)
1¼ ounces Real Hacienda 100 Percent Blue Agave Añejo tequila
¾ ounce Grand Marnier
1½ ounces freshly squeezed lemon juice or lime juice
Ice**

✶

Run the lemon or lime wedge around the rim of a hurricane-style Margarita glass. Dip the rim of the glass into the saucer of salt, rotating the rim in the salt until the desired amount has collected on the glass.

Measure the tequila, Grand Marnier, and lemon or lime juice into a 16-ounce cocktail shaker glass full of ice. Place a stainless steel cocktail shaker over the glass, tapping the top to create a seal. Shake vigorously for about 5 seconds and pour into the salt-rimmed glass.

✶*Margarita Tip* *Another great way of serving Margaritas at parties is a Margarita punch bowl: simply transpose the ingredients in any recipe from ounces to parts. Pour all the ingredients into a punch bowl, mix well, then add a large block of ice. Stir often. Provide a ladle and allow your guests to serve themselves in pre-salted glasses.*

✶*Tequila Tidbit* *While there are 360 different varieties of agave, blue agave is the only one which tequila can be made from. The word agave is derived from the Greek for noble — which seems highly appropriate to us!*

58

# Hussong's

*Hussong's describes itself as a 99 percent blue agave reposado tequila. According to the label, "Juan Hussong built the cantina (Hussong's in Ensenada, Mexico) in 1892 to accommodate fortune-seeking stagecoach riders. The cantina has since become a mecca for travelers from around the world who come to seek good times and good friends. In their search they discover still another treasure — a rare tequila that for many years was a well-hidden secret."*

*A manager at Hussong's claimed that Hussong's actually is 100 percent blue agave, but that in order to comply with Mexican government regulations, it cannot claim to be 100 percent because it is shipped to the United States in bulk and bottled by the McCormick Distilling Company of Weston, Missouri.*

# Hussong's Special Margarita

Makes 1 Margarita

*At Hussong's cantina in Ensenada, their Margaritas are made by mixing equal parts of Hussong's tequila, Cointreau, and lemon juice, and are served over ice in a salt-rimmed glass.*

**1 lemon or lime wedge**
**Saucer of kosher salt (about ¼-inch deep)**
**1¼ ounces Hussong's 99 Percent Agàve tequila**
**¾ ounce Cointreau**
**1½ ounces freshly squeezed lemon juice or lime juice**
**Ice**

Run the lemon or lime wedge around the rim of a hurricane-style Margarita glass. Dip the rim of the glass into the saucer of salt, rotating the rim in the salt until the desired amount has collected on the glass.

Measure the tequila, Cointreau, and lemon or lime juice into a 16-ounce cocktail shaker glass full of ice. Place a stainless steel cocktail shaker over the glass, tapping the top to create a seal. Shake vigorously for about 5 seconds and pour into the salt-rimmed glass.

★*Margarita Tip A great party idea is to organize a blind tasting of tequilas and/or Margaritas for your friends. Pour drinks made with a different tequila (both silver and gold), and compare notes. Make sure that guests arriving by car have designated drivers — they can be put in charge of pouring the drinks, coding them so guests don't know ahead of time the brands they are trying, and announcing the results.*

★*Tequila Tidbit The golden hue found in most aged tequilas (reposado, añejo, and muy añejo) comes from the oaken barrels in which the original white tequila is placed. The more aging the tequila has does not necessarily mean the darker gold it will be. The intensity of the color is dependent on both the duration of the aging process, as well as the type of oak barrel that is used.*

# Herradura

*Herradura is estate-bottled by the Romo family in the foothills of the Sierra Madre mountains of Jalisco. The estate dates back to 1870, and Herradura tequila has been produced by five successive generations. Besides being the first super-premium tequila imported into the United States, Herradura Gold has long served as a quality standard for the Mexican tequila industry.*

# The Silver Herradura Margarita

Makes 1 Margarita

*Herradura was one of the first 100 percent agave tequilas to come into the United States and still is the number one selling super-premium brand in the country.*

**1 lemon or lime wedge**
**Saucer of kosher salt (about ¼-inch deep)**
**1¼ ounces Herradura Silver Natural tequila**
**¾ ounce Bols triple-sec**
**1½ ounces freshly squeezed lemon juice or lime juice**
**Ice**

Run the lemon or lime wedge around the rim of a hurricane-style Margarita glass. Dip the rim of the glass into the saucer of salt, rotating the rim in the salt until the desired amount has collected on the glass.

Measure the tequila, triple-sec, and lemon or lime juice into a 16-ounce cocktail shaker glass full of ice. Place a stainless steel cocktail shaker over the glass, tapping the top to create a seal. Shake vigorously for about 5 seconds and pour into the salt-rimmed glass.

★ *Margarita Tip* *The size of the ice is an important factor in creating the perfect Margarita (see page 20). Supermarket or liquor store ice is usually small enough, but if the cubes are larger than 1 inch square, make sure to crack them into smaller pieces.*

★ *Tequila Tidbit* *We like the rich, natural flavor of Bols triple-sec, but there are other brands on the market. If you are considering buying another brand, be sure to read the label. We recommend only investing in a triple-sec that uses the natural flavors of exotic oranges and orange peel. Definitely avoid those that contain artificial flavors.*

# The Santiago Margarita

Makes 1 Margarita

*This Margarita was inspired by a longtime Maria's patron named James (Santiago translates as St. James in English) who wanted to improve on an existing Margarita, The Rafael (see page 41). James suggested that we substitute Herradura 100 percent Blue Agave Silver tequila for the Cuervo Gold, and whaddya know, he helped us create one of the most elegant and smoothest Margaritas around.*

★

**1 lemon or lime wedge
Saucer of kosher salt (about ¼-inch deep)
1¼ ounces Herradura Silver Natural tequila
¾ ounce Cointreau
1½ ounces freshly squeezed lemon juice or lime juice
Ice**

★

Run the lemon or lime wedge around the rim of a hurricane-style Margarita glass. Dip the rim of the glass into the saucer of salt, rotating the rim in the salt until the desired amount has collected on the glass.

Measure the tequila, Cointreau, and lemon or lime juice into a 16-ounce cocktail shaker glass full of ice. Place a stainless steel cocktail shaker over the glass, tapping the top to create a seal. Shake vigorously for about 5 seconds and pour into the salt-rimmed glass.

★ *Margarita Tip* It is a common misconception that Margaritas were invented to cool off the heat of chiles in Mexican food. Not so — in fact, a lot of Mexican food isn't hot at all. On the other hand, since most New Mexican, modern Southwestern, and Tex-Mex food is picante, perhaps the Margarita does make a nice alternative to beer when eating our wonderful regional fare.

★ *Tequila Tidbits* The Tequila Producers Association (La Camera Regional de la Industria Tequilera) was formed in 1949 and has fewer than 30 members. Headquartered in Guadalajara, it is the trade group which promotes tequila throughout the world and helps maintain the highest standards of production.

# The Herradura Gold Margarita

### Makes 1 Margarita

*Back when tequila in the United States was exclusive to the Southwest because the East Coast hadn't yet discovered it, tequila aficionados would brag about the smooth, outstanding flavor of Herradura Gold. These folks would never use this wonderful nectar in a Margarita – "sorry," they'd say, "this is sippin' stuff." Well, we think this "sippin' stuff" makes an awesome Margarita.*

★

**1 lemon or lime wedge**
**Saucer of kosher salt (about ¼-inch deep)**
**1¼ ounces Herradura 100 Percent Blue Agave Natural Gold tequila**
**¾ ounce Cointreau**
**1½ ounces freshly squeezed lemon juice or lime juice**
**Ice**

Run the lemon or lime wedge around the rim of a hurricane-style Margarita glass. Dip the rim of the glass into the saucer of salt, rotating the rim in the salt until the desired amount has collected on the glass.

Measure the tequila, Cointreau, and lemon or lime juice into a 16-ounce cocktail shaker glass full of ice. Place a stainless steel cocktail shaker over the glass, tapping the top to create a seal. Shake vigorously for about 5 seconds and pour into the salt-rimmed glass.

★*Margarita Tip The glasses we use for our real Margaritas are made by the Libbey Glass Company. The hurricane-style, 13¼-ounce "rocks" glasses are called Poco Grande II. The saucer-type glasses are Coupette/Margarita. They can be ordered from a good kitchen store or any Libbey Glass dealer.*

★ *Tequila Tidbit The blue agave flavor of Herradura Gold is enhanced by aging in oak barrels which imparts a light golden hue to the tequila. Herradura Silver Natural is a premium tequila, produced from 100 percent blue agave, with no additives.*

# The Herradura Añejo Margarita

Makes 1 Margarita

*Herradura was the first 100 percent blue agave tequila to be imported into the United States and effectively marketed, which gave it a head start on other super-premium brands. This is probably the main reason why it is just about the best-known of the super-premium tequilas available; some tequila fans would say that this is the finest tequila available. The rich, flavorful taste of Herradura añejo tequila is enhanced by two full years of aging.*

**1 lemon or lime wedge**
**Saucer of kosher salt (about ¼-inch deep)**
**1¼ ounces Herradura Añejo tequila**
**¾ ounce Cointreau**
**1 ½ ounces freshly squeezed lemon juice or lime juice**
**Ice**

Run the lemon or lime wedge around the rim of a hurricane-style Margarita glass. Dip the rim of the glass into the saucer of salt, rotating the rim in the salt until the desired amount has collected on the glass.

 Measure the tequila, Cointreau, and lemon or lime juice into a 16-ounce cocktail shaker glass full of ice. Place a stainless steel cocktail shaker over the glass, tapping the top to create a seal. Shake vigorously for about 5 seconds and pour into the salt-rimmed glass.

★ *Margarita Tip* If fresh lemons or limes are not available for squeezing, we suggest you use the commercial bottled Realemon, which is generally available in most grocery stores. Realemon is pure lemon juice with a small amount of preservative added; however, once opened, the shelf-life is limited — two or three days in the refrigerator at most, so be prepared to use it up or throw the rest away.

★ *Tequila Tidbit* The blue agave plant is a succulent and not a cactus, as some people would have you believe. It is kin to the aloe vera plant. (Maybe that explains why 100 percent agave tequila is so smooth!)

# El Viejito

*El Viejito means "the little old man." Simple, right? Wrong. The official name of this 100 percent blue agave tequila is El Viejito 100 Percent Blue Agave Produccion de Aniversario Tequila Reposado! It is aged in American oak barrels and has a fresh agave smell and a great agave flavor.*

# El Viejito Margarita

## Makes 1 Margarita

*Somehow, El Viejito tequila seems to be one of the most authentic examples of the wonderful Mexican product that we import: the label is not too flashy, although the bottle is very elegant in a humble sort of way.*

**1 lemon or lime wedge**
**Saucer of kosher salt (about ¼-inch deep)**
**1¼ ounces El Viejito 100 Percent Blue Agave tequila**
**¾ ounce Cointreau**
**1½ ounces freshly squeezed lemon juice or lime juice**
**Ice**

Run the lemon or lime wedge around the rim of a hurricane-style Margarita glass. Dip the rim of the glass into the saucer of salt, rotating the rim in the salt until the desired amount has collected on the glass.

Measure the tequila, Cointreau, and lemon or lime juice into a 16-ounce cocktail shaker glass full of ice. Place a stainless steel cocktail shaker over the glass, tapping the top to create a seal. Shake vigorously for about 5 seconds and pour into the salt-rimmed glass.

★ *Margarita Tip Different tequilas, as well as different combinations of triple-sec, Cointreau, and Grand Marnier are what make Margaritas so flexible. The different possibilities make experimenting with Margaritas so much fun.*

★ *Tequila Tidbit As you drive to Tequila from the city of Guadalajara (Mexico's second largest city), you begin to understand why they named the* Tequilana weber, *"blue agave." On either side of the narrow, two-lane asphalt highway is acre after acre of neat rows of huge agave plants. In the breeze, these noble plants create an ocean of brilliant azure as the sun highlights the blue green color of their swordlike leaves.*

# El Tesoro

El Tesoro tequilas are arguably the finest tequilas of all. They are made from estate-grown agave only, and every piña is hand-selected at peak ripeness. Each piña is harvested when it is individually mature, rather than when most of the agaves in one field or another are ready. The piñas are then cut, roasted in steam ovens for two days, and squeezed with a huge millstone to extract the sweetness. The juice is then transferred by hand to vats, fermented, then double-distilled to the exact proof desired. El Tesoro is literally fermented to proof; the miel, or agave juice, is poured into fermenting vats with the exact amount of yeast to begin the fermentation process. It is one of the most flavorful of all tequilas because nothing else is added. This makes El Tesoro one of the purest forms of alcoholic beverage made today.

# The Elizabeth II Margarita

## Makes 1 Margarita

*One of Maria's cocktail waitresses, Elizabeth, was explaining to a customer when a Margarita was mixed using the premium El Tesoro tequila and Grand Marnier, the latter dominated the tequila, while a Margarita made with El Tesoro and Cointreau allowed the flavor to emerge more fully. The customer was a Grand Marnier lover, however, and asked Elizabeth if the bartender would be willing to mix a Margarita using El Tesoro, a half measure of Grand Marnier, and a half measure of Cointreau. It proved to be a winning combination, and the name Elizabeth II stuck, referring to one Elizabeth and two orange liqueurs. For as long as I can remember, anyone who has ordered an Elizabeth II once has ordered it again.*

★

**1 lemon or lime wedge**
**Saucer of kosher salt (about ¼-inch deep)**
**1¼ ounces El Tesoro Plata Tequila**
**½ ounce Grand Marnier**
**½ ounce Cointreau**
**1½ ounces freshly squeezed lemon juice or lime juice**
**Ice**

★

Run the lemon or lime wedge around the rim of a hurricane-style Margarita glass. Dip the rim of the glass into the saucer of salt, rotating the rim in the salt until the desired amount has collected on the glass.

Measure the tequila, Grand Marnier, Cointreau, and lemon or lime juice into a 16-ounce cocktail shaker glass full of ice. Place a stainless steel cocktail shaker over the glass, tapping the top to create a seal. Shake vigorously for about 5 seconds and pour into the salt-rimmed glass.

★*Margarita Tip* We prefer additive-free, coarse-grained kosher salt to regular table salt, but table salt can be substituted — just moisten the rim of the glass very lightly with the lemon or lime wedge.

★ *Tequila Tidbit* All El Tesoro tequilas are 100 percent blue agave, handmade, and double-distilled at precisely the right time to produce an 80-proof liquor (40 percent alcohol by volume). Most other distilled spirits either have distilled water added to lower the proof or alcohol added to raise the proof.

# Maria's Famous La Ultima Margarita

## Makes 1 Margarita

*This is one of the very first super-premium Margaritas to be marketed in the world. Up until this particular Margarita, most tequila connoisseurs would only drink their precious 100 percent super-premium nectar straight. There should be no substituting any of the ingredients in this Margarita. Taste them all together and I'm confident that you will find it will live up to its name,*
*"The Ultimate Margarita."*

**1 lemon or lime wedge**
**Saucer of kosher salt (about ¼-inch deep)**
**1¼ ounces El Tesoro 100 Percent Blue Agave Plata tequila**
**¾ ounce Cointreau**
**1½ ounces freshly squeezed lemon juice or lime juice**
**Ice**

Run the lemon or lime wedge around the rim of a hurricane-style Margarita glass. Dip the rim of the glass into the saucer of salt, rotating the rim in the salt until the desired amount has collected on the glass.

Measure the tequila, Cointreau, and lemon or lime juice into a 16-ounce cocktail shaker glass full of ice. Place a stainless steel cocktail shaker over the glass, tapping the top to create a seal. Shake vigorously for about 5 seconds and pour into the salt-rimmed glass.

★*Margarita Tip This Margarita regularly spawns debate with tequila connoisseurs who accuse us of violating the integrity of the tequila by using it in a Margarita. So, you be the judge. Sip a little El Tesoro Plata on its own. Then make up this Margarita and taste it. Which is more pleasant? I think the Margarita is so much more enjoyable than even the best tequila (I rarely drink tequila straight anymore).*

★*Tequila Tidbit Maria's pours more El Tesoro tequila than any other restaurant or bar in America. Our Maria's Famous La Ultima Margarita is responsible for this.*

# The Grand Platinum Margarita

Makes 1 Margarita

*This Margarita is made with two of the most expensive distilled spirits available: 100 percent blue agave El Tesoro Plata (silver) tequila and Grand Marnier. You do get what you pay for, though. Here is a world-class cocktail that is probably one of the purest, most natural concoctions you can enjoy. El Tesoro is handmade and double-distilled to proof, while Grand Marnier is triple-distilled from exotic oranges and peels with premium cognac added. And of course, the lemon juice is freshly squeezed from one of nature's most efficient and remarkable containers.*

**1 lemon or lime wedge**
**Saucer of kosher salt (about ¼-inch deep)**
**1¼ ounces El Tesoro 100 Percent Blue Agave Plata tequila**
**¾ ounce Grand Marnier**
**1½ ounces freshly squeezed lemon juice or lime juice**
**Ice**

Run the lemon or lime wedge around the rim of a hurricane-style Margarita glass. Dip the rim of the glass into the saucer of salt, rotating the rim in the salt until the desired amount has collected on the glass.

Measure the tequila, Grand Marnier, and lemon or lime juice into a 16-ounce cocktail shaker glass full of ice. Place a stainless steel cocktail shaker over the glass, tapping the top to create a seal. Shake vigorously for about 5 seconds and pour into the salt-rimmed glass.

★ *Margarita Tip In addition to Realemon as a substitute for fresh lemon or lime juice, Minute Maid produces a frozen nonconcentrated, pure lemon juice which has no additives. Under no circumstances should you use a sweetened lemon or lime juice such as frozen lemonade or frozen limeade. With the added sugar in these products, you'll end up with an icky-sweet Margarita that's a waste of good tequila.*

★ *Tequila Tidbit During the Mexican Revolutionary War earlier this century, a popular drinking song among the troops featured tequila: Si porque tomo tequila, Mañana tomo jerez. Si porque me ves borracho, Mañana ya no me ves. Roughly translated: "So I'm drinking tequila, tomorrow, I'll drink sherry wine. If you see me drunk, tomorrow you won't see me at all."*

# The Grand Treasure Margarita

Makes 1 Margarita

*Tequila lovers who have tried most of the 100 percent blue agave tequilas on the market generally have their own preferred "sipping" tequila. El Tesoro Muy Añejo ("very aged") tequila is certainly a contender for the title of Best Tequila in the World (let's not pull any punches). This is a tequila to enjoy in a brandy snifter after dinner. Try it sometime — you'll think you're sipping a fine cognac. This Margarita combines Muy Añejo tequila with Grand Marnier, which is popular with those who enjoy a heavier alcohol taste rather than the subtle agave flavor of silver tequilas.*

**1 lemon or lime wedge**
**Saucer of kosher salt (about ¼-inch deep)**
**1¼ ounces El Tesoro Muy Añejo 100 Percent Blue Agave tequila**
**¾ ounce Grand Marnier**
**1½ ounces freshly squeezed lemon juice or lime juice**
**Ice**

Run the lemon or lime wedge around the rim of a hurricane-style Margarita glass. Dip the rim of the glass into the saucer of salt, rotating the rim in the salt until the desired amount has collected on the glass.

Measure the tequila, Grand Marnier, and lemon or lime juice into a 16-ounce cocktail shaker glass full of ice. Place a stainless steel cocktail shaker over the glass, tapping the top to create a seal. Shake vigorously for about 5 seconds and pour into the salt-rimmed glass.

★ *Margarita Tip At Maria's, we think tequila should be drunk in Margaritas, so we strongly discourage shots and slammers — we believe folks have a tendency to over-indulge when drinking tequila this way. We prefer our guests to drink liquor because they like it, not because they want to get drunk.*

★ *Tequila Tidbit Even though the golden El Tesoro Muy Añejo tequila is hand-made, double-distilled to proof and then carefully aged in oak barrels for more than two years, I personally prefer the "fresh," newly distilled plata (or silver) El Tesoro. The aging process seems to cause the tequila to abandon the deep agave flavor that is so unique to super-premium 100 percent blue agave tequila.*

# La Margarita del Joven Esteban

Makes 1 Margarita

*We named this Margarita after one of Maria's longtime waiters, Steve Young (joven means "young"), who couldn't understand why we didn't have a Margarita on our list that combined the El Tesoro Muy Añejo and Cointreau. After all, we had both El Tesoro plata and El Tesoro Añejo Margaritas mixed with Grand Marnier. Steve conned us into believing that his customers insisted on El Tesoro Muy Añejo and Cointreau Margaritas (which they did — after a little coaching from Steve). Since we believe that the customer is always right, and because we heard rave reviews from the customers drinking this concoction, we decided to add it to our Real Margarita List and name it after Steve.*

**1 lemon or lime wedge**
**Saucer of kosher salt (about ¼-inch deep)**
**1¼ ounces El Tesoro 100 Percent Blue Agave Muy Añejo tequila**
**¾ ounce Grand Marnier**
**1½ ounces freshly squeezed lemon juice or lime juice**
**Ice**

Run the lemon or lime wedge around the rim of a hurricane-style Margarita glass. Dip the rim of the glass into the saucer of salt, rotating the rim in the salt until the desired amount has collected on the glass.

Measure the tequila, Grand Marnier, and lemon or lime juice into a 16-ounce cocktail shaker glass full of ice. Place a stainless steel cocktail shaker over the glass, tapping the top to create a seal. Shake vigorously for about 5 seconds and pour into the salt-rimmed glass.

★ *Margarita Tip As in any culture, in Mexico there are all kinds of toasts to make when enjoying a drink with friends. Some toasts are simply translations from one language to another. The most common toast in the Spanish language is Salud (which accompanied with the lifting of a Margarita glass, means "to your health").*

★ *Tequila Tidbit We are sometimes asked whether the rumor is true that tequila is an aphrodisiac. Well, we like to think it is, but alas, there is no scientific evidence (yet) to support our wishful thinking.*

# Patrón

Patrón is one of the great new entries into the U.S. super-premium 100 percent blue agave market. You know you're in for a treat the minute you see the unique hand-blown reusable decanter-type bottle, complete with a cork-lined hand-blown glass stopper. On the other hand, there's no free lunch, as they say, and though this is an outstanding tequila, Patrón is generally a little higher priced than others of comparable quality, almost certainly because of their superior packaging. If you have a use for the decanter, Patrón is a particular bargain; if not, you will be paying for it anyway — you be the judge.

TEQUILA
100% AGAVE

TEQUILA

PATRÓN

PRODUCED & BOTTLED IN MEXICO
SOLE IMPORTER:
ST. MAARTEN SPIRITS, LTD.
CULVER CITY, CA 90232

750
ML

ALC./VOL.
(80 PROOF)

# La Margarita de La Patróna

Makes 1 Margarita

*This Margarita is made with Patrón Silver — a 100 percent blue agave tequila from the highlands of Jalisco (an area that is increasingly touted by tequila experts as the prime agave-growing region of Mexico). Patrón in Spanish means "boss," and la patrona is the feminine version, or loosely translated, "boss lady" — so here we present "the boss lady's Margarita."*

**1 lemon or lime wedge**
**Saucer of kosher salt (about ¼-inch deep)**
**1¼ ounces Patrón 100 Percent Blue Agave Silver tequila**
**¾ ounce Cointreau**
**1½ ounces freshly squeezed lemon juice or lime juice**
**Ice**

✶

Run the lemon or lime wedge around the rim of a hurricane-style Margarita glass. Dip the rim of the glass into the saucer of salt, rotating the rim in the salt until the desired amount has collected on the glass.

Measure the tequila, Cointreau, and lemon or lime juice into a 16-ounce cocktail shaker glass full of ice. Place a stainless steel cocktail shaker over the glass, tapping the top to create a seal. Shake vigorously for about 5 seconds and pour into the salt-rimmed glass.

✶ *Margarita Tip* Here's another toast offered in Mexico (imported from Spain); this one's a little more elaborate than the simple Salud: Salud, dinero y amor, y tiempo para gustarlos. ("Health, money, and love, and the time to enjoy them.")

✶ *Tequila Tidbit* By the early 1990s, tequila had become the tenth best-selling spirit in the United States, at 5.1 million cases (vodka is the market leader). Tequila is also the fastest-growing spirit in terms of sales, largely because of the ever-increasing popularity of Margaritas.

75

# The Don Roberto Margarita

Makes 1 Margarita

*This Margarita is named after Bob Noyes, a former partner of ours at Maria's, both because he is a patrón — one of the bosses — but also because this is his favorite Margarita. It features Patrón Añejo tequila, which like the silver version (page 75) is bottled in hand-blown glass decanter-type bottles.*

★

**1 lemon or lime wedge**
**Saucer of kosher salt (about ¼-inch deep)**
**1¼ ounces Patrón 100 Percent Blue Agave Añejo tequila**
**¾ ounce Cointreau**
**1½ ounces freshly squeezed lemon juice or lime juice**
**Ice**

★

Run the lemon or lime wedge around the rim of a hurricane-style Margarita glass. Dip the rim of the glass into the saucer of salt, rotating the rim in the salt until the desired amount has collected on the glass.

Measure the tequila, Cointreau, and lemon or lime juice into a 16-ounce cocktail shaker glass full of ice. Place a stainless steel cocktail shaker over the glass, tapping the top to create a seal. Shake vigorously for about 5 seconds and pour into the salt-rimmed glass.

★ *Margarita Tip Since the word tequila refers to the volcanic lava hills of the Jalisco region, we decided to experiment with a Volcano Margarita, made with dry ice (to create the volcano smoke) and Tabasco (for the heat). All the other ingredients — tequila, triple-sec, and lemon juice — were as usual. It was awful. The moral of this tale is that you can experiment all you want, but not everything you try to make into a Margarita is going to be a true delight.*

★ *Tequila Tidbit All Patrón tequila is made with large stone milling wheels that squeeze all the juices from the steam-cooked agave piñas. The fermentation process includes the pressed piña fibers, which the manufacturer claims help impart the unique flavor and smoothness. The fermented liquid is then double-distilled and hand-bottled. The quality of this particular tequila as well as the unique packaging make this one of our favorite gifts for housewarmings, holidays, or just special friends.*

# Centinela

Centinela is another handmade
100 percent blue agave tequila,
and it's produced and bottled at the
distillery in the mountains near
Arandas, in the state of Jalisco.
Centinela has been produced for
more than one hundred years and
is available in four forms: plata, or
blanco, white tequila; reposado,
which is aged for three months;
añejo, which is aged for one year,
and añejo tres años, their
top-of-the-line tequila which is
aged for three years.

# The Centinela Reposado Margarita

Makes 1 Margarita

*Centinela is distributed in the United States by El Dorado Importers, based in Santa Rosa, New Mexico and is probably the best value of all the super-premium tequilas being imported to the U.S.*

★

**1 lemon or lime wedge**
**Saucer of kosher salt (about ¼-inch deep)**
**1¼ ounces Centinela 100 Percent Blue Agave Reposado tequila**
**¾ ounce Cointreau**
**1½ ounces freshly squeezed lemon juice or lime juice**
**Ice**

★

Run the lemon or lime wedge around the rim of a hurricane-style Margarita glass. Dip the rim of the glass into the saucer of salt, rotating the rim in the salt until the desired amount has collected on the glass.

Measure the tequila, Cointreau, and lemon or lime juice into a 16-ounce cocktail shaker glass full of ice. Place a stainless steel cocktail shaker over the glass, tapping the top to create a seal. Shake vigorously for about 5 seconds and pour into the salt-rimmed glass.

★*Margarita Tip* Here's another fun taste test. Splurge on a bottle of each of the different types of tequila made by one producer, such as Centinela. Make Margaritas using identical ingredients except for the different forms of the one brand of tequila and compare notes.

★*Tequila Tidbit* Mezcal is not tequila. We can call mezcal a cousin to tequila because it is made from the same agave plant. However, mezcal is only distilled once and is not, unlike tequila, subject to any governmental regulations.

# The Silver Sentinel Margarita

Makes 1 Margarita

*Centinela is from the same region as El Tesoro (same climate and same soil conditions) and can be favorably compared with any 100 percent blue agave tequila. The plata Centinela used in this Margarita is smooth, with a dry-sweet taste.*

**1 lemon or lime wedge**
**Saucer of kosher salt (about ¼-inch deep)**
**1¼ ounces Centinela 100 Percent Blue Agave Plata tequila**
**¾ ounce Cointreau**
**1½ ounces freshly squeezed lemon juice or lime juice**
**Ice**

Run the lemon or lime wedge around the rim of a hurricane-style Margarita glass. Dip the rim of the glass into the saucer of salt, rotating the rim in the salt until the desired amount has collected on the glass.

Measure the tequila, Cointreau, and lemon or lime juice into a 16-ounce cocktail shaker glass full of ice. Place a stainless steel cocktail shaker over the glass, tapping the top to create a seal. Shake vigorously for about 5 seconds and pour into the salt-rimmed glass.

★*Margarita Tip It can be fun to experiment with tequilas and other fruit-based liquors or juices. For example, a Melon Margarita made with tequila, Midori, and lemon juice; a Watermelon Margarita using watermelon juice instead of lemon juice; an Apple Margarita made with apple juice. Use cranberry juice, mango nectar — there's no limit. See the next chapter for some recipes along these lines.*

★*Tequila Tidbit The ancient Mexican Indian cultures handled drunkenness (usually caused by drinking too much pulque) by shaving the perpetrator's head — the sign of disgrace — for the first offense. The second offense was a little more harsh — death!*

# The Blue Angel Margarita

### Makes 1 Margarita

*Way back when, some enterprising individual decided to make a blue Margarita, and the only obvious way to do that was to use blue Curaçao instead of triple-sec. Blue Curaçao is an orange liqueur made from the juice and peel of Curaçao oranges with blue food coloring added. This makes a fun cocktail, and the Blue Angel Margarita is one of the few drinks at Maria's that contains any artificial ingredients.*

★

**1 lemon or lime wedge**
**Saucer of kosher salt (about ¼-inch deep)**
**1¼ ounces Centinela 100 Percent Blue Agave Plata tequila**
**¾ ounce Bols Blue Curaçao (or add blue food coloring to triple-sec)**
**1½ ounces freshly squeezed lemon juice or lime juice**
**Ice**

★

Run the lemon or lime wedge around the rim of a hurricane-style Margarita glass. Dip the rim of the glass into the saucer of salt, rotating the rim in the salt until the desired amount has collected on the glass.

Measure the tequila, blue Curaçao, and lemon or lime juice into a 16-ounce cocktail shaker glass full of ice. Place a stainless steel cocktail shaker over the glass, tapping the top to create a seal. Shake vigorously for about 5 seconds and pour into the salt-rimmed glass.

★ *Margarita Tip* It's no wonder that Margaritas are associated with good times and wonderful memories — it's a tradition. A passage from a book called Tequila, lo Nuestro (published by Sauza) reads in translation: "In every drop of tequila, of our tequila, there is a spirit of the hospitality of our land and the promise of a fiesta. Of a fiesta that ever ends. The fiesta of the tequila." Well, since the key ingredient in a Margarita is tequila, it stands to reason that good times can be expected from drinking them.

★ *Tequila Tidbit* As mentioned earlier, the reason the blue agave is so called is because of the bluish hue that the fields of the plants give as they undulate along the hillsides of the Sierra Madre range. The juices of these plants are not, as some suppose, blue — in fact, once they have been fermented and double-distilled into tequila, they are crystal clear.

# The Hundred Grand Margarita

Makes 1 Margarita

*When we first taste-tested this Margarita using Centinela's Añejo tequila, it was so smooth and the tequila flavor was so alive that we thought we had used Cointreau instead of Grand Marnier. This is a reflection of the fine taste of this particular tequila, and backs our contention that Centinela Añejo is one of the best tequilas available in the United States.*

**1 lemon or lime wedge**
**Saucer of kosher salt (about ¼-inch deep)**
**1¼ ounces Centinela 100 Percent Blue Agave Añejo tequila**
**¾ ounce Grand Marnier**
**1½ ounces freshly squeezed lemon juice or lime juice**
**Ice**

Run the lemon or lime wedge around the rim of a hurricane-style Margarita glass. Dip the rim of the glass into the saucer of salt, rotating the rim in the salt until the desired amount has collected on the glass.

Measure the tequila, Grand Marnier, and lemon or lime juice into a 16-ounce cocktail shaker glass full of ice. Place a stainless steel cocktail shaker over the glass, tapping the top to create a seal. Shake vigorously for about 5 seconds and pour into the salt-rimmed glass.

★ *Margarita Tip As mentioned earlier, Grand Marnier often tends to overwhelm the flavor of the tequila in a Margarita. However, when you use Grand Marnier with the right tequila — like Centinela's Añejo — there is no better Margarita in the world.*

★ *Tequila Tidbit When visiting Mexico, you may hear the agave plant referred to as Maguey. It is still the same plant, the agave Tequilana weber, blue variety. Maguey is what the Spanish explorers called agave when they first came into the tequila country.*

# The Centinela Añejo Margarita

Makes 1 Margarita

*Just as the smooth agave tones of this aged tequila come through when mixed with Grand Marnier (see previous recipe), so too do they blend wonderfully well with Cointreau.*

✳

**1 lemon or lime wedge**
**Saucer of kosher salt (about ¼-inch deep)**
**1¼ ounces Centinela 100 Percent Blue Agave Añejo tequila**
**¾ ounce Cointreau**
**1½ ounces freshly squeezed lemon juice or lime juice**
**Ice**

✳

Run the lemon or lime wedge around the rim of a hurricane-style Margarita glass. Dip the rim of the glass into the saucer of salt, rotating the rim in the salt until the desired amount has collected on the glass.

Measure the tequila, Cointreau, and lemon or lime juice into a 16-ounce cocktail shaker glass full of ice. Place a stainless steel cocktail shaker over the glass, tapping the top to create a seal. Shake vigorously for about 5 seconds and pour into the salt-rimmed glass.

✳ *Margarita Tip  In Spanish, the word Margarita also means "daisy." If you know anyone called Margarita, you can call her Daisy just to show off your phenomenal knowledge, but forget about going into a bar and ordering a "Daisy." They will only think you're strange (and bartenders don't take well to strange folk) and you'll never get your Margarita!*

✳ *Tequila Tidbit  The word mezcal is derived from the words* metl *and* xalli, *which mean "stew" or "concoction" in the ancient language of the Nahuatl Indian tribe.*

# El Amor de Oro Margarita

Makes 1 Margarita

*The name of this drink, one of the most elegant Margaritas in the world, is translated to mean "The Golden Love."*

✳

**1 lemon or lime wedge**
**Saucer of kosher salt (about ¼-inch deep)**
**1¼ ounces Centinela 100 Percent Blue Agave Tres Años tequila**
**¾ ounce Cointreau**
**1½ ounces freshly squeezed lemon juice or lime juice**
**Ice**

✳

Run the lemon or lime wedge around the rim of a hurricane-style Margarita glass. Dip the rim of the glass into the saucer of salt, rotating the rim in the salt until the desired amount has collected on the glass.

Measure the tequila, Cointreau, and lemon or lime juice into a 16-ounce cocktail shaker glass full of ice. Place a stainless steel cocktail shaker over the glass, tapping the top to create a seal. Shake vigorously for about 5 seconds and pour into the salt-rimmed glass.

✳ *Margarita Tip* An aged tequila can be savored in a snifter glass, as a fine cognac would, and sipped lovingly. Centinela 100 Percent Blue Agave Tres Años is aged for 3 years in oak barrels (by law, añejo tequila must be aged at least 1 year). This extra aging gives the liquor a rich golden hue and one of the deepest agave flavors of all tequilas on the market.

✳ *Tequila Tidbit* Once the blue agave plant has reached maturity, it must be harvested to be used for tequila production. If it is not harvested immediately upon maturity, the piña will sprout a long-stemmed flower which grows about two feet a day (right out of the center) and can reach a height of 6 to 12 feet. Once this occurs, the agave is no longer usable for tequila, as the plant has spent its energy (in the form of the sugar) to create this incredible flower.

# Chapter 5

# More Magnificent Tequila Drinks

**T**equila isn't *just* for Margaritas. This next chapter includes some bar favorites that use tequila but are not Margaritas, as well as one "Margarita" that doesn't use tequila.

## ★ Magnificent Tequila Drinks ★

The Strawberry Margarita

The Peach Margarita

The Absolut Margarita

The Lucero de la Mañana

The Gulf Breeze

The Bloody Maria

The Chimayó Cocktail

Tequila Sunrise

Sangrita

# The Strawberry Margarita

Makes 1 cocktail

*This may not be a real Margarita, but it sure as heck is a first cousin. Some of the most fun you can have with tequila (other than with Margaritas) is the way you can mix it with fresh fruit and juices. As far as we're concerned, that's the only time a "frozen Margarita" is justified. ✄ Let your imagination run wild when making fruit Margaritas. The possibilities are almost endless — bananas, mangoes, papayas — but our favorites are Margaritas made with strawberries and peaches (see page 87). Always use fresh fruit if you can, but if it's out of season, use unsweetened individually frozen fruits. We also recommend using simple syrup rather than the sugary citrus sweet-and-sour mix that most bars use in their so-called Margaritas.*

✳

**1¼ ounces José Cuervo Silver tequila**
**¾ ounce Bols triple-sec**
**1½ ounces freshly squeezed lemon juice**
**2 ounces simple syrup or sweet-and-sour mix**
**6 to 8 stemmed fresh or partially thawed frozen strawberries,
plus 1 fresh strawberry for garnish (optional)**
**2 cups cracked ice**

✳

Place all of the ingredients into a blender and blend until smooth. Pour the mixture into a hurricane-style Margarita glass. For a garnish, cut a strawberry three-fourths up from its tip and place on the rim of the glass if you wish.

**To Make Simple Syrup:**

Heat equal parts of sugar and water to boiling point. When sugar has dissolved, remove from heat and cool. Keep in a capped bottle. Does not need refrigeration.

# The Peach Margarita

Makes 1 cocktail

*Use the ripest, juiciest peaches you can find and slice them over the blender, so you don't waste a drop of the nectar. As with the preceding recipe, use unsweetened individually frozen peaches if the fresh fruit is out of season, but avoid sweetened frozen peaches as the drink will be too sweet. Be careful — these fruit cocktails are so delicious and flavorful that you tend to forget they contain alcohol.*

**1¼ ounces José Cuervo Silver tequila**
**¾ ounce Bols triple-sec**
**1½ ounce freshly squeezed lemon juice**
**2 ounces simple syrup (see page 86) or sweet-and-sour mix**
**1 peeled, pitted, and sliced fresh peach or ¾ cup partially frozen peach slices**
**2 cups cracked ice**

Place all of the ingredients into a blender and blend until smooth. Pour mixture into a hurricane-style Margarita glass.

# The Absolut Margarita

Makes 1 cocktail

*We all know people who insist that they're allergic to whatever it is they don't like (or don't want to try). One regular customer at Maria's would watch us experimenting with Margaritas, but when we offered to let her try a sip, she claimed to be allergic to tequila. So we came up with this cocktail for our customer so she could drink Margaritas without drinking tequila. This may not be a "real" Margarita, but you'll still enjoy it.*

**1 lemon or lime wedge
Saucer of kosher salt (about ¼-inch deep)
1¼ ounces Absolut vodka
¾ ounce Cointreau
1½ ounces freshly squeezed lemon juice or lime juice
Ice**

★

Run the lemon or lime wedge around the rim of a hurricane-style Margarita glass. Dip the rim of the glass into the saucer of salt, rotating the rim in the salt until the desired amount has collected on the glass.

Measure the vodka, Cointreau, and lemon or lime juice into a 16-ounce cocktail shaker glass full of ice. Place a stainless steel cocktail shaker top over the glass, tapping the top to create a seal. Shake the drink vigorously for about 5 seconds and pour it into the salt-rimmed glass.

# The Lucero de la Mañana

Makes 1 cocktail

*This is one of the most refreshing eye-openers you could imagine. The name of the cocktail is a pun on its creator's name (your humble author) and the Spanish translation is "morning star." It'll certainly be the star of your next breakfast or brunch party. Remember: the fresher and colder the orange juice, the better the drink.*

Ice
1¼ ounces El Tesoro Plata tequila
8 ounces freshly squeezed orange juice
Splash of cranberry juice
1 lime or orange slice for garnish (optional)

Fill a 16-ounce tumbler with ice. Pour the tequila over the ice. Add the orange juice and stir. Add the cranberry juice and serve. If desired, garnish with a lime or orange slice.

# The Gulf Breeze

Makes 1 cocktail

*This drink is the kissin' cousin of the previous cocktail. Same idea, different fruit juice. Remember, the colder the juice is, the better.*

**Ice**
**1 ¼ ounces El Tesoro Plata tequila**
**8 ounces freshly squeezed grapefruit juice**
**Splash of cranberry juice**
**1 lime or orange slice for garnish (optional)**

Fill a 16-ounce tumbler with ice. Pour the tequila over the ice. Add the grape-fruit juice and stir. Add the cranberry juice and serve. If desired, garnish with a lime or orange slice.

# The Bloody Maria

Makes 1 cocktail

*Look again! Yes, it's Bloody Maria rather than Mary, and if you've already figured out that we use tequila rather than vodka, go to the head of the bartending class! Be sure to follow our recipe exactly, and more than likely you'll agree it's the best Bloody Maria or Mary you've ever had.*

**Ice**
**1 ounce José Cuervo Silver tequila**
**2 lime wedges (each one-eighth of a lime)**
**1 quick shot Worcestershire sauce**
**7 dashes Tabasco sauce**
**Salt and black pepper to taste**
**1 cup tomato juice (preferably Sacramento brand)**

Fill a 16-ounce tumbler three-quarters full of ice. Pour the tequila over the ice. Squeeze one of the lime wedges into the glass. Add the Worcestershire sauce and the Tabasco (use less if you prefer) and shake a generous amount of salt and pepper into the glass. Fill the glass with tomato juice and stir vigorously. Float the juice from the second squeezed lime wedge over the top of the mixture. Run the squeezed lime wedge around the rim of the glass and drop it into the mixture. Do not stir again.

Sprinkle more salt and pepper on top of the mixture and on the rim of the glass so that a little sticks, then serve.

# The Chimayó Cocktail

Makes 1 cocktail

*Chimayó is an old village in a valley of the Sangre de Cristo mountains that was originally settled by the Spanish in the seventeenth century. It's located about 30 miles north of Santa Fe and remains a charming place that's well known for the healing properties of the holy dirt in the santuario (or church). Chimayó is also famous for its outstanding New Mexican red chiles, probably the best chile in the world, as well as for its delicious red apples. The Jaramillo family invented this cocktail to promote the village and its apples, many of which are harvested in the orchards around their famous restaurant — the picturesque Rancho de Chimayó.*

**Ice**
**1¼ ounces Herradura Silver tequila**
**¼ ounce crème de cassis**
**1 ounce fresh apple cider or apple juice**
**¼ ounce freshly squeezed lemon juice**
**1 red apple wedge**

Fill a double old-fashioned glass with ice. Pour the tequila, crème de cassis, apple cider or juice, and lemon juice over the ice, and stir. Garnish the glass with an apple wedge and serve.

# Tequila Sunrise

Makes 1 cocktail

*After the Margarita, the Tequila Sunrise is perhaps the oldest and most popular tequila drink. As with all of these recipes, the better the ingredients, the better the final product. Use freshly squeezed juice and a good tequila; if ordering this at a bar or restaurant, be sure to avoid the house "well" brand, unless you know it's a premium tequila like Cuervo or Sauza (Cuervo Silver is the "well" brand at Maria's).*

**Ice**
**6 ounces freshly squeezed orange juice**
**1¼ ounces José Cuervo Silver tequila**
**Splash of grenadine**
**1 lime or orange wedge, or 1 maraschino cherry on a toothpick, for garnish (optional)**

✳

Fill a double old-fashioned glass three-quarters full of ice. Add the orange juice and tequila, and stir. Add the grenadine. Garnish the glass with a fruit wedge or cherry, if desired, and serve.

# Sangrita

Makes 8 cocktails

*We do not promote the drinking of tequila in shots with a lick of salt and a bite of lime because that's how people get drunk. A decent tequila can go down so smoothly that some folks drink way too much, way too quickly for their own good. This can also be a waste of good tequila. Anyone drinking alcohol for any reason other than enjoyment should get help — no one should drink to "get drunk."*  *Okay, we're down from our soapbox now. The Sangrita, a classic Mexican drink, is a fun way to enjoy an occasional shot of tequila; it seems to go best as an eye-opener before brunch. Great for hangovers!*

✴

**1 lime wedge
Saucer of kosher salt (about ¼-inch deep)
6 ounces tomato juice (preferably Sacramento brand)
1 ounce freshly squeezed orange juice
1 ounce freshly squeezed grapefruit juice
½ ounce freshly squeezed lime juice
8 dashes Tabasco sauce, or to taste
Salt and black pepper to taste
New Mexico red chile powder
1 shot tequila**

Run the lime wedge around the rim of 8 individual shot glasses. Dip the rim of the glasses into the saucer of salt, rotating the rim in the salt until the desired amount has collected on the glass.

In a large glass, mix the juices together. Add the Tabasco sauce and sprinkle salt and pepper over the mixture and stir. Pour the mixture into the shot glasses. Sprinkle a little chile powder on top and serve with a shot of your favorite tequila. Drink the tequila and immediately drink the Sangrita as a chaser.

# Chapter 6

# Maria's New Mexican Kitchen

## *Food to Serve with Margaritas*

If you're going to the trouble of making Margaritas with some of the wonderful tequilas we've described earlier, you may as well go whole hog and rustle up some New Mexican classics for the table. Somehow, the two go together perfectly, as we've discovered at Maria's. The recipes that follow are simple, straightforward, and truly represent the Southwestern cuisine of Old Santa Fe.

### ★ Food to Serve with Margaritas ★

New Mexico Family-Style Tacos
Maria's World-Famous Salsa
Guacamole
Classic Posole
Maria's Blue Corn Enchiladas
Maria's Frijoles
Al's Cheddar Cheese and Onion Bean Dip

# New Mexico Family-Style Tacos

Makes 6 servings (12 tacos)

*This simple recipe can be halved, doubled, tripled, or whatever. The recipe was designed for soft tacos (kept warm by covering them with a cloth), but the crisp U-shaped taco shells are a treat, as well. You can add a bowl of sour cream, guacamole, or different taco sauces or salsas according to your fancy.*

**1 pound extra-lean ground beef**
**Vegetable oil for frying**
**12 yellow or blue corn tortillas**
**½ head iceberg lettuce, coarsely chopped**
**1 yellow onion, coarsely chopped**
**2 ripe tomatoes, coarsely chopped**
**2 cups (8 ounces) shredded Cheddar cheese**
**Maria's World-Famous Salsa (see page 99) or your favorite taco sauce or salsa**
**Salt and pepper to taste**

In a large skillet or sauté pan, sauté the ground beef until cooked through and browned. Drain off fat and place the beef in a large serving bowl.

In another skillet or sauté pan, heat about ½ inch of vegetable oil until very hot. Fry a tortilla for about 5 to 10 seconds or just until softened, holding it with cooking tongs. Do not allow the tortilla to become crisp.

Place the tortilla on a paper towel on a serving plate and repeat until all the tortillas are fried, layering paper towels between them to absorb the oil. If not serving immediately, cover the tortillas with a clean dish towel to keep warm.

Place the lettuce, onion, tomatoes, cheese, and taco sauce or salsa in separate serving bowls in the center of the table along with the meat and tortillas. Place a tortilla on a serving plate, spoon some beef on the center of the tortilla, add taco sauce, salt, and pepper, then sprinkle a little onion, tomato, cheese, and lettuce on top of the beef (in that order). Fold the tortilla to form a soft taco, pick it up, and eat.

★ *Note:* *All ingredients listed in these recipes are assumed to be of medium size, unless otherwise stated. For most of the typical New Mexican-grown ingredients, see "Sources" for mail-order availability.*

# Maria's World-Famous Salsa

Makes about 3 cups

*This is a great taco sauce for the preceding recipe,
and it is ideal with corn tortilla chips.*

★

**2 cups chunky tomato sauce**
**1 cup chopped New Mexico green chiles**
**½ cup water**
**½ teaspoon salt**
**1 tablespoon minced garlic**
**¼ cup diced yellow onion**
**2 tablespoons crushed red chile flakes or chile powder**

★

Combine all the ingredients well in a mixing bowl and adjust seasoning to taste.
Cover and chill. Keep refrigerated for up to after three days.

# Guacamole

Makes about 6 cups

*Some things were made to go together. Guacamole, corn tortilla chips, and Margaritas, for example, have a natural affinity. We believe that guacamole, like Margaritas, must be made by hand. The other secret of great guacamole is to use the ripest Haas avocados you can find; they're the wrinkly ones with the deep, dark, purplish-green color. This recipe will create a dip that's guaranteed to go fast and avoid leftovers!*

**6 ripe Haas avocados, peeled and pitted**
**½ cup chopped New Mexico green chiles**
**1 yellow onion, finely chopped**
**1 ripe firm tomato, finely diced**
**4 garlic cloves, minced**
**Dash of Worcestershire sauce**
**Juice of ½ lemon**
**Salt to taste**
**Tortilla chips**

In a large stainless steel or ceramic bowl, mash the pitted avocado with a fork, leaving chunks no larger than ½-inch across.

Add the green chile, onion, tomato, and garlic, and blend together.

Blend in the Worcestershire sauce and lemon juice (being careful to strain any seeds).

Add salt. Serve with corn tortilla chips. If not serving immediately, place an avocado pit in the center of the dip, cover the bowl with plastic wrap, and refrigerate. This will minimize the oxidation that turns the surface of guacamole brown.

# Classic Posole

Makes 6 to 8 servings

*To make this recipe, you must use posole corn — an Indian corn typically found in New Mexico. Check with your favorite store or grocer to see if it's available before attempting this recipe. Posole is a hearty soup that is a traditional Christmas dish in New Mexico, although it's served year-round at Maria's and in most New Mexican restaurants. It's particularly appropriate for inclusion here because it originated in Jalisco — the center of the tequila country.*

**1 pound dried posole corn**
**4 quarts water**
**2 cups diced yellow onions**
**1 cup fresh pork rind (hogback), cut into 1 inch squares**
**2 cups diced (¾-inch cubes) lean pork**
**1 tablespoon minced garlic**
**1 tablespoon salt**
**1 cup coarsely crushed, seeded, and stemmed dried New Mexico red chiles**

Rinse the posole in cold water. Place in a large (at least 8-quart) stew pot and cover with the water.

Add the onions and pork. Bring to a boil, cover, reduce the heat, and cook at a rolling boil for at least 1 hour, or until the posole has popped like popcorn.

Reduce the heat to a simmer and add the garlic, salt, and red chiles (add more water if the broth has reduced).

Simmer for 30 minutes. Serve in large soup bowls.

# Maria's Blue Corn Enchiladas

Makes 4 servings

*Grind your own dried New Mexico red chiles or use pure New Mexico red chile powder for this recipe. Any other chile powder is just not the same. To make a vegetarian chile sauce, just eliminate the ground beef.*

*Red Chile Enchilada Sauce:*
**2 tablespoons vegetable shortening or lard**
**9 heaping tablespoons New Mexico red chile powder**
**4 quarts cold water**
**1 heaping tablespoon all-purpose flour**
**4 garlic cloves, minced**
**1 teaspoon salt**

**2 pounds extra-lean ground beef**

*Enchiladas:*
**Vegetable oil for frying**
**12 blue, yellow, or white corn tortillas**
**Red Chile Enchilada Sauce, above**
**2 cups coarsely chopped onions**
**2 cups coarsely chopped tomatoes**
**4 cups (1 pound) shredded Cheddar cheese**
**½ head iceberg lettuce, shredded**

**To prepare the Red Chile Enchilada Sauce:**

In a large saucepan, melt the shortening or lard over medium-high heat until just smoking.

Add the chile powder, 1 tablespoon at a time, whisking constantly to avoid lumping.

When too thick to whisk, add ½ cup of the water. Heat a little, and continue to add the chile powder, alternating with the water until all the water and all the chile powder have been combined.

In a small bowl, mix the flour with a little water until the flour is dissolved. Add this flour-water mixture to the chile powder mixture and bring to a light boil.

Stir in the garlic and salt. Set aside and keep warm.

**To prepare the beef:**

In a large skillet or sauté pan, sauté the ground beef until medium rare.

Drain off the fat and add the ground beef to the chile sauce.

Cook for 45 minutes to 1 hour, stirring occasionally.

**To prepare the Enchiladas:**

Preheat the oven to 200°F.

Heat about ½ inch of vegetable oil in a medium skillet until very hot. Fry one tortilla at a time for about 5 to 10 seconds, or just until softened. Do not allow tortillas to become crisp. Drain excess oil by holding tortillas with tongs over the pan.

Drop one tortilla into Red Chile Enchilada Sauce to saturate, then place it flat on a deep individual oven-proof plate or dish.

Sprinkle some of the onions, tomatoes, and cheese over the tortilla, and top with an additional ¼ cup of the chile sauce.

Saturate a second tortilla in Red Chile Enchilada Sauce and place it over the first. Top with onions, tomatoes, and cheese and another ¼ cup of the chile sauce.

Top with a third tortilla (the tortillas will look like a stack of pancakes covered with red chile sauce). Spoon chile sauce over the top of the stack and sprinkle with cheese.

Place the tortilla stack in preheated oven. Repeat the procedure for 3 more serving plates or dishes. Serve at once, garnished with the lettuce and remaining chopped tomatoes, and accompanied with your favorite Margarita.

# Maria's Frijoles

Makes about 8 cups

*This bean recipe is so easy, so inexpensive, and so delicious that it should become a staple in anyone's repertoire of Southwestern food. It's also the perfect base for refried beans (see below). Use only pinto beans for this recipe, and ask for "new crop" if you have a choice. Never leave a pot of beans to cook while you leave the house; they could go dry and burn (it's happened).*

**1 pound dried pinto beans**
**4 quarts water**
**6 ounces salt pork, cut into ½-inch cubes**

Thoroughly sort through the beans to remove any foreign objects such as stones or twigs. Rinse beans under cold water and place in a large (at least 8-quart) stew pot covered with the water. Soak for 1 to 2 hours, or overnight.

Add the salt pork to the beans and soaking water and bring to a rolling boil. Reduce the heat and simmer, uncovered, for at least 2 hours or until tender enough to mash. Add more water if at any time the beans are covered by less than 2 inches. Stir from time to time to make sure the beans are not sticking to the bottom of the pot. The longer the beans cook, the better they are.

*Vegetarian frijoles:* Replace the salt pork with 2 tablespoons of vegetable shortening and add salt during the last 30 minutes of cooking (adding salt earlier will make the beans tough).

*Refried Beans:* Mash the drained, cooked beans with a fork and simmer in hot bacon fat or vegetable oil for about 10 minutes, stirring constantly.

# Al's Cheddar Cheese and Onion Bean Dip

Makes about 8 cups

*Here's a great bean dip that uses ingredients that are available just about anywhere. It's easy to make and virtually foolproof, but it does require some time and effort to prepare, as well as a chafing dish, fondue dish, or some kind of heated serving apparatus to keep the dip warm (a crockpot set at its lowest setting would also work). You can make a smaller amount of the dip by dividing the recipe by half.*

**1 tablespoon solid vegetable shortening**
**4 cups drained Maria's Frijoles (see page 104) (reserve the broth)**
**1 large onion, diced**
**3 garlic cloves, finely minced**
**1 cup Maria's World-Famous Salsa (see page 99) or other** *picante* **tomato-based salsa**
**1 cup chopped New Mexico green chiles**
**4 cups (1 pound) shredded Cheddar cheese**
**Tortilla chips**
★

In a large skillet or sauté pan, melt the shortening over medium-high heat. Add the beans and mash them while frying. Lower the heat and continue to fry mashed beans until heated through.

Transfer beans to a larger saucepan, adding the onion, garlic, salsa, and green chile. Cook over medium heat, stirring constantly.

Slowly add cheese, stirring to blend (if the mixture becomes too thick, add a little of the reserved bean broth).

Once the mixture is blended smoothly, transfer to a chafing dish, fondue dish, or crockpot. Serve with tortilla chips.

# Tequila Glossary

★ **José Cuervo Silver** *The reigning king of tequilas! This is the number one best-selling tequila in the United States. If your liquor store or grocery store does not stock Cuervo Silver, it's time to change stores! Cuervo Silver is the tequila which Maria's pours from the "well" — that is, any tequila drink that is requested without specifying the brand. This tequila is not 100 percent blue agave, but it is considered a premium tequila. There's hardly anything to choose between José Cuervo and Sauza when it comes to mass-produced, unaged white tequila, but my vote, by a hair, goes to Cuervo.*

★ **Cuervo Especial (Gold)** *The label says "Cuervo Especial" but this is the one that is commonly referred to as "Cuervo Gold." However, all the gold refers to is caramel coloring, which is added to maintain a consistent color to the liquid to emulate añejo (aged) gold tequila. Cuervo Especial is a premium tequila, but it is not aged and is not 100 percent blue agave. This is the second best-selling premium tequila at Maria's, after Cuervo Silver.*

★ **Cuervo 1800** *A premium, less than 100 percent blue agave tequila, the label on the bottle describes it as "a natural golden distillate from the agave plant." This tequila, like José Cuervo Silver and Cuervo Especial is made in Tequila, Jalisco. It comes in an attractive, reusable decanter bottle.*

★ **Dos Reales de Plata** *José Cuervo produces this entry into the super-premium tequila market without any reference (other than the NOM number) to the fact that it is a Cuervo product. While this silver tequila is not a 100 percent blue agave tequila, the label reads, "Dos Reales Plata is a tequila of unparalleled flavor and quality. It is distilled from selected agave plants to achieve the perfect balance of traditional tequila flavor and extra smoothness." We'll go along with that!*

★ **Dos Reales Añejo** *The golden sister of Dos Reales Plata, this, too, is one of José Cuervo's new entries into the premium tequila market. Here again, there is no reference to José Cuervo anywhere on the label or bottle. This tequila is labeled añejo and since Cuervo is generally considered the heart and soul of the Mexican tequila industry, you can bet your bottom peso that this is indeed an aged-in-oak product, even though the color is a little darker than most añejos.*

★ *Cuervo Tradicional* José Cuervo's very best tequila, Cuervo Tradicional is a 100 percent blue agave reposado tequila. Due to limited production, Cuervo Tradicional is bottled in 375 ml bottles (half the size of the regular 750 ml tequila bottles). This tequila has the light-golden hue of a true reposado tequila and the aroma of blue agave.

★ *Sauza Silver* Sauza claims that this is the "traditional favorite and largest selling tequila in Mexico." (Cuervo claims the same for the United States.) This grand tequila is more than adequate for anybody's Margarita bar, even though it is not 100 percent blue agave. As with most silver or white tequilas, this is a "fresh" tequila with little or no aging.

★ *Sauza Tequila Extra (Gold)* Nowhere on the label of Sauza Tequila Extra is there a reference to gold or any aging process. Like Cuervo Gold, this premium tequila is colored with caramel to give it the golden color. It is not 100 percent blue agave, but it is readily available throughout the United States.

★ *Sauza Tres Generaciones* Literally "Three Generations," referring to the founding fathers of the Sauza company: Don Cenobio, Don Eladio, and Don Javier Sauza. This premium tequila is not 100 percent blue agave. However, the careful distilling of this exquisite tequila and its aging in oak creates an unparalleled smoothness and richness, and qualifies it to be called añejo (aged).

★ *Sauza Conmemorativo* Conmemorativo is considered by Sauza as their flagship brand. This wonderful premium tequila is aged in oak to give it a soft golden color. It is not 100 percent blue agave, but it is one of the finest and smoothest añejo tequilas imported from Mexico. Readily available throughout the United States.

★ *Sauza Hornitos* Not Sauza's most expensive tequila, but perhaps their best. Hornitos is 100 percent blue agave and a reposado tequila, aged in oak for at least three months to give it a light golden hue. Hornitos is available throughout the United States.

★ *La Viuda de Romero Reposado* Literally "Widow of Romero," this is a premium tequila, but is not 100 percent blue agave. Viuda de Romero is aged for six months in oak barrels, hence the light golden coloring. The super-premium brands from this distillery are imported under the name of Real Hacienda — the entire line of which is 100 percent blue agave.

★ *La Viuda de Romero Añejo* Unlike La Viuda de Romero Reposado, La Viuda de Romero Añejo is aged for two years in oak barrels. This premium tequila is not 100 percent blue agave.

★ *Real Hacienda Premium Silver* This is a 100 percent blue agave tequila, produced from agave which has been grown in the Tequila region by the Viuda de Romero family for the past century.

★ *Real Hacienda Reposado* This is a light golden 100 percent blue agave reposado tequila. It is aged for six months in oak barrels, which gives this super-premium tequila just a hint of oak flavor. As of late, this tequila is rapidly gaining wider and wider distribution outside of Mexico.

★ *Real Hacienda Añejo* As with the other Real Hacienda products, this outstanding 100 percent blue agave tequila is distilled by La Viuda de Romero. It is aged in small oak barrels for at least two years, which results in its deep golden coloring.

★ *Hussong's 99 Percent Agave Tequila* The label suggests that this reposado tequila is made by the founder and operator of Hussong's Cantina in Ensenada, Baja, Mexico, and claims that it is made from 99 percent blue agave. The label (NOM number) also tells us that the tequila is in fact made by the same folks who produce El Viejito tequila. This is a great tequila and comes in an attractive stoneware vessel.

★ *Herradura Silver Natural Tequila* The first of the super-premium 100 percent blue agave tequilas to be popularized in the United States, Herradura is still held dearly in the hearts of those who discovered it long before other 100 percent blue agave tequilas reached the market. This silver tequila is unaged, and made in the same general area as Cuervo and Sauza, in Amatitan, just outside the village of Tequila. By regulation, Herradura Silver tequila is bottled at the distillery and exported in the bottle. All Herradura tequilas are readily available throughout the United States.

★ *Herradura Gold Natural Tequila* The golden hue of the distilled 100 percent blue agave is evidence that this outstanding tequila has been aged in oak under the regulation set forth by the Mexican government. Like the Herradura Silver, this was the first tequila of its type to have been imported into the United States.

★ *Herradura Añejo Natural Tequila.* Up until the late 1980s, Herradura Añejo Tequila was the undisputed champion of all the super-premium tequilas imported into the United States. For many years, this 100 percent blue agave tequila was the only tequila of its kind to be widely available in the United States. Now, it has some stiff competition in the marketplace .

★ *El Viejito Reposado Tequila* This 100 percent blue agave reposado tequila is lighter in color compared to El Viejito Tequila Añejo. However, it is a deeper golden color than most reposados. El Viejito Reposado is generally available throughout the United States.

★ *El Viejito Tequila Añejo* Certified by the Mexican Government to be aged in oak barrels for a period of at least a year, this 100 percent blue agave tequila is a super-premium that can be enjoyed as sipping tequila as well as used in Margaritas.

★ *El Tesoro de Don Felipe Plata* *This is our personal favorite of all tequilas. The major reason: an aroma that instantly signals 100 percent blue agave and a flavor that is pure, rich, and distinctive. It's no wonder that this tequila is so outstanding. Each agave piña used to make El Tesoro is estate-grown on Don Felipe's own acreage, in the mountainous region of Los Altos. I consider this the benchmark of all silver tequilas.*

★ *El Tesoro de Don Felipe Muy Añejo* *This tequila is handmade the same as El Tesoro Plata and aged in oak barrels for two years then aged two years further in Don Felipe's stone cellars. El Tesoro's aging process gives a golden color to the liquid while imparting an elegance and smoothness unparalleled in the industry. El Tesoro Muy Añejo is available in most areas of the United States and distribution is growing rapidly.*

★ *Patrón Silver* *This outstanding 100 percent blue agave tequila is not only hand-made and exported from Mexico, but the bottles are beautiful: one-of-a-kind hand-blown decanters complete with glass stoppers. Each bottle is hand-numbered and signed to certify its hand-bottling and is marketed in Mexico under the name Tequila Siete Leguas (Seven Leagues).*

★ *Patrón Añejo* *This tequila is aged in small oak barrels for at least two years. Its golden color is naturally derived from this aging process; no caramel food coloring is added. Like the silver, it is exported in hand-blown glass decanter-style bottles. Patrón is becoming more widely available, especially in the western United States.*

★ *Centinela Tequila Blanco* *This 100 percent blue agave reposado tequila is gently aged for about three months to provide a slight golden tint and character to its flavor. The agave grown in the highlands region of Los Altos, Jalisco where Centinela is located has a unique flavor and its tequila offers an interesting taste alternative to brands made in the foothills of the Tequila region of Jalisco. Centinela has limited but growing distribution in the United States, as it has only recently begun to be imported.*

★ *Centinela Tequila Añejo* *This golden 100 percent blue agave tequila has been aged in oak by one of the older producers in the Los Altos area of Jalisco. The careful attention paid to the traditional method of natural fermentation and the manufacturing by hand make this one of the better añejos available in the United States.*

★ *Centinela Tres Años (Muy Añejo)* *This top-of-the-line 100 percent blue agave Centinela tequila is handmade, like the blanco, reposado, and añejo, and aged longer — three years in oak — to create one of the best tequilas in the world.*

# Resources

Following is a listing of importers and/or distributors of tequilas and other products called for in the recipes throughout *Maria's*. If you can't find one of the tequilas or other products mentioned in this book at your local grocery or liquor store, simply call, write, or fax one of the sources listed below and ask for the nearest dealer.

Please bear in mind that as in all industries, changes in the tequila industry occur constantly. While it is our intent to provide you with the most current, up-to-date source list, all infomation following is subject to change.

★ **Centinela** *Eldorado Importers, 761 Parker Ave., Santa Rosa, New Mexico 88435 (800) 468-0672*

★ **Cointreau** *Rémy Amerique, Inc., Cointreau Division, 1350 Avenue of the Americas, 7th Floor, New York, New York 10019 (212) 399-4200*

★ **El Tesoro** *Robert Denton & Co., 2724 Auburn Rd., Auburn Hills, Michigan 48326 (800) 669-7808 FAX (313) 299-3836*

★ **El Viejito** *Paterno Imports, 4242 N. Capistrano, Unit No. 128, Dallas, Texas 75287 (214) 733-0240 FAX (214) 733-0072; and Paterno Imports, 2701 S. Western Ave., Chicago, Illinois 60608 (312) 247-7070*

★ **Grand Marnier** *Carillon Importers, Ltd., Glenpointe Center West, Teaneck, New Jersey 07666 (201) 836-7799*

★ **Herradura** *Sazerac Co., Inc., P.O. Box 52821, New Orleans, Louisiana 70152-2821 (504) 831-2383 FAX (504) 831-2383*

★ **Hussong's** *McCormick Distilling Co., 1 McCormick Lane, Weston, Missouri 64098 (816) 640-2276 Hussong's Cantina SAA de CV, Ave Ruiz No. 113, Encenada, Mexico, BC 22800*

★ **José Cuervo** *José Cuervo International, Inc., 25950 Acero, Suite 250, Mission Viejo, California 92691 (714) 583-7755*

★ **La Viuda Romero** *Mina International Services, 9034 N. 23rd Ave., Suite 13, Phoenix, Arizona 85021 (602) 943-9311*

★ **Patrón** *St. Maarten Spirits, Ltd., 8460 Higuera, Culver City, California 90232 (800) 723-4767 FAX (310) 841-2335*

★ *Real Hacienda* Mina International Services, 9034 N. 23rd Ave., Suite 13, Phoenix, Arizona 85021    (602) 943-9311

★ *Sauza* Domecq Importers, Inc., 143 Sound Beach Ave., Old Greenwich, Connecticut 06870    (800) 697-6547    FAX (203) 637-6595

★ *Margarita Glasses* Libbey Glass, Inc., 940 Ash St., Toldeo, Ohio 43693 (419) 729-7272

★ *New Mexican Cooking Ingredients* Bueno Foods, 2001 4th St. SW, Albuquerque, New Mexico 87102    (800) 95-CHILE